TEO
CURTIS

THEY STILL SPEAK

Readings for the Lesser Feasts

✠

EDITED BY

J. Robert Wright

CHURCH HYMNAL CORPORATION

New York

Table of Contents

✠

Introduction

✠

The purpose of this book is to provide a reading by or about every person commemorated in the Calendar of Lesser Feasts of the Episcopal Church that will be suitable for public liturgical use or for private meditation. First preference has normally been given to materials written in their own words by the persons themselves. In the few cases where such material has not been available or appropriate, a reading about the person has generally been taken from a descriptive source that is near in time to that person's life. Of the Calendar's 132 lesser feasts, all of which are provided for in this volume, well over a hundred of these readings are, or include, the actual words of the people themselves, while the other selections (about twenty-five) were chosen from the best contemporary descriptive sources when authentic original quotations were not available.

This book is, first of all, intended to be a companion to the Book of Common Prayer and to the volume entitled *Lesser Feasts and Fasts*. Readings for the Major Feasts of the Book of Common Prayer, as well as additional selections written by some of the persons in the Lesser Calendar, are cross-indexed at the end of this volume from the author's *Readings for the Daily Office from the Early Church* (Church Hymnal Corporation, 1991), to which the present volume is also intended as a companion. Hymns written by these persons that can be used as alternate readings are also cross-indexed from *The Hymnal 1982*. In the case of one particular commemoration, Bishop Samuel Seabury, two readings are given, one more appropriate for his consecration (1784) and one for his teaching.

Introduction

The use of these readings allows the persons commemorated in the Calendar "still to speak," as much as possible, in their own words and especially on their own feast days, in passages that are not only authentic examples of their writing or teaching but also personal and verbal messages from them to us in our present pilgrimage. Such a reading can serve as the basis for a homily at the Eucharist on the feast day of the person commemorated, or in place of the homily itself, or as a spoken anthem following the Reading(s) and before the Gospel, or as a meditation (public or private) before or after any service on the given day. In the Daily Office, where such readings are authorized on p. 142 of the 1979 American Book of Common Prayer, one of these selections can follow after the lesson or lessons from Holy Scripture, or can come in place of the hymn or anthem following the Collects. These selections are not intended to replace the reading of, or preaching on, Holy Scripture appointed for the day, but only to supplement it and deepen its application. They are intended, however, as is the Calendar itself, to help make "the communion of saints" a living reality here and now.

There are presently 132 commemorations of Lesser Feasts in the Calendar of the Episcopal Church, and we may well ask: Where did these names come from and upon what principles are they included? The addition of names to a standard list ("canon") for liturgical commemoration has a long history, beginning with the sporadic local commemorations in the early patristic period. This process intensified after Constantine's official recognition of the Christian church in the early fourth century brought a deeper sense of historical consciousness and a thirst for tangible evidences of holiness. Although already in the New Testament the martyrs were being singled out for special honor (Rev. 6:9-11, 17:6), the earliest recorded instance of the church gathering to celebrate a day of martyrdom "as a birthday" is probably that of Polycarp, in the year 156 (see the reading for February 23). In time, the *foci* of devotion related to these celebrations came to include relics in the

West and icons in the East. Gradually a process of centralization developed for such commemorations in the Western Church, and Ulrich of Augsburg in 993 was the first person to be canonized by a procedure that increasingly centered on the See of Rome. Although some local canonizations continued for a while, papal canonization soon became and then remained the norm until the time of the Reformation in the sixteenth century, and there was a considerable multiplication of lesser feasts in the calendars of the service books of the later Middle Ages. Reverence or veneration for the saints (*dulia;* and for Mary *hyperdulia*) increasingly became confused with the worship *(latreia)* due to God alone, in spite of the clear distinctions made earlier in the patristic church (cf. *Readings for the Daily Office from the Early Church*, pp. 224, 247, 337, and 414). On the eve of the Reformation, the Sarum missal that was commonly used in England provided for commemoration of some 175 saints.

In what can now be seen as an over-reaction to the medieval multiplication of saints and their days, the first English Prayer Book of 1549 swept away all of these commemorations save twenty-four persons mentioned by name in the New Testament (Our Lord and the Apostles, the Evangelists, and a few others), who were designated in the Prayer Book calendar by the color red. In the next Prayer Book, 1552, four post-New Testament figures were added, and in that of 1662 there were some sixty-seven of these "Black Letter" days (distinguished from the twenty-four days of New Testament saints, which were still printed in red). All of the Black Letter days were eliminated from the first American Prayer Book of 1789, but the principle of observing such "lesser" feasts has gradually re-asserted itself. With the American Prayer Book of 1979, in addition to the "major" commemorations, the number of "lesser" ones was placed at 120. As of the present writing, the number of the latter has been increased to 132. It is noteworthy that by no means all of these persons are "Anglicans," however one may choose to define the term.[1] The Church of England's *Alterna-*

tive Services Book in 1980 put the number at 83,[2] and the total for the Lesser Calendar of the *Lutheran Book of Worship* (1978) has been counted at 141.[3]

For the Episcopal Church, it takes the vote of two successive General Conventions to make changes in the Lesser Calendar, and persons dead for less than fifty years are generally considered ineligible unless, like Martin Luther King, Jr. and Jonathan Daniels, they are considered to have died by martyrdom.[4] Considerable discussion of the whole process and principles of calendar revision occurred in the General Convention of 1991, where the number was increased to 132 and a review of the criteria for selection was mandated. Although a set of criteria does exist for the inclusion of additional commemorations, adopted by the General Convention in 1988 and reaffirmed by it in 1991,[5] they are not intended for "the making of saints" as is the case with even the revised procedure followed in the Roman Catholic Church. The present total of such persons who have passed this process in the Church of Rome now numbers over 4500, including all beatified as well as those canonized, and of these nearly 600 have been added by Pope John Paul II, who revised extensively the Roman Catholic process in 1983.[6] The Orthodox Eastern Churches make no distinction between beatification and canonization, and they have a process for canonization that is less specific than that of the Church of Rome.[7]

The Prayer Book Calendar of the Episcopal Church reserves the term "saint" for persons named in the New Testament, although elsewhere in the Prayer Book of 1979 four other, post-New Testament persons are so designated. (St. Chrysostom, pp. 72, 102, St. Francis, pp. 812, 833, Saint Athanasius, p. 864, and Saint Augustine, p. 873; cf. pp. 18, 195, 198, 246, 250). A strong case can be made that all baptized Christians are "saints," or at least are called to be saints, that is, to be holy persons (the Latin *sanctus* means "holy" in English), by reason of their baptisms (cf. II Timothy 1:9). From this premise it can further be maintained that all the figures of the "lesser" calendar also deserve to be called "saints" in the sense of being persons designated by the church (i.e., "canonized") as examples of that holiness to which we are all called, even if not in the technical and quantifiable sense still used for such designations in the Church of Rome. That the Episcopal Church, in its own modest way, accords the veneration or reverence of *dulia* to the saints and *hyperdulia* to Mary, and allows them to be invoked for their prayers,[8] can be seen in its 1982 Hymnal, nos. 269, 282–3, and 618, and in its Eucharistic canon D and intercession form V. Visible *foci* of such devotion that are increasingly evidenced in Episcopal churches include icons as well as statues and relics. It is this context of veneration, in turn, that undergirds the mystical communion of the pilgrim church on earth with those who have gone before and now live with God in heaven.

Many volumes of church history have been combed in the research and preparation of this volume. Where feasts of the Episcopal Church are the same as those in the Roman Catholic Church, use has often been made here of the corresponding selections from *The Liturgy of the Hours* authorized in that church following the revision of its Divine Office mandated by the Second Vatican Council. Appreciation is also hereby expressed to the various copyright holders listed under "Acknowledgments" for their permission to use or edit certain of the selections that have been printed here.

For the present book, fresh translations of Greek and Latin sources have been done in many cases, and emendations, contractions, and alterations to the readings have often been made for editorial purposes. On occasion, some material has been omitted between the beginning and ending of some selections. In order to facilitate reading with fewer distractions, the style of the International Commission on English in the Liturgy, which prepared or sponsored the new translations used in the Roman Catholic Church, has generally been followed in *not* using ellipsis points to indicate omissions in the text. Such omissions can be ascertained precisely by consulting the pages given in the source references. Brackets have been employed within the texts to indicate words supplied by the editor for the sake of clarity. In translations from patristic and medieval sources, human gender language, which was always more flexible in the original Greek and Latin, has been made more inclusive along the principles established by the *New Revised Standard Version* of the Bible. In post-medieval sources written originally in the English language, only some modernization of spelling, capitalization, and punctuation, but not inclusivity of gender, has been feasible. Passages from Scripture, even though they may be paraphrases or otherwise inexact quotations, have been translated or reproduced as they appear in the works themselves instead of being conformed to some standard modern text. Rather more ample introductory sentences and datings have been provided for many of the lesser-known readings from the modern period. The arrangement of selections in this volume commences, not with the beginning of the civil calendar year on January 1 but (as in the Book of Common Prayer itself) with the start of the church's liturgical year in Advent. Source references are given at the end of each selection for easy location in an original work or scholarly edition, although especially in the case of translations from Greek and Latin the reference given may not necessarily be the immediate source of the particular version that is used or adapted here. Full bibliographical references for common scholarly abbreviations are not usually provided. The year-dates at the top headings of each reading are those of the person's death, as in the official Calendar of the Episcopal Church, except that for the consecration of Samuel Seabury. Further discussion of editorial principles and of translation questions may be found in the appendix to the second and subsequent printings of *Readings for the Daily Office from the Early Church.*

A great number of friends, some old and some new, have helped me to track down and locate several of the readings I have chosen for this volume, and I wish now to record my thanks to them, in alphabetical order, as well as to any others whom I may have forgotten to mention: Dorothy Anderson, Owanah Anderson, D. Barrington Baltus, John Borelli, Franklin M. Cooper, Roger Corless, Kortright Davis, Noel W. Derbyshire, Rozanne Elder, Deirdre Good, David Green, Charles R. Henery, Brother Kenneth, Charles Long, Krikor Maksoudian, John Morris, Louise Pirouet, Paul Reeves, Paul Richardson, John Rowe, John Ryan, David Sellery, Philip Turner, Geoffrey Wainwright, William C. Wantland, Frederick B. Williams, and Franklin M. Wright.

✠✠✠✠✠✠✠

The several persons who "still speak" in this volume are the primary figures in all of church history whom the Episcopal Church currently chooses to remember publicly and to commemorate liturgically on an annual basis. Both the unity of church history and the ecumenical diversity of Christian witness within it are vividly manifested by these readings. It is therefore my pleasure to dedicate this book in honor of three great bishops who in recent years have perceived and embodied the ecumenical vision of the Episcopal Church in their teaching and in their episcopal ministries. These are their names and dioceses:

BISHOP JOHN H. BURT OF OHIO,

BISHOP DAVID B. REED OF KENTUCKY,

BISHOP EDWARD W. JONES OF INDIANAPOLIS

Each in succession has chaired in recent years the Standing Commission on Ecumenical Relations of the Episcopal Church, and under them I have been privileged to serve that commission as a member and consultant. Their enthusiastic and persistent leadership in matters ecumenical for the sake of the church's unity, their equanimity of concern for all Christians of every church throughout the pages of history even as I continue to teach it in seminary, and their catholicity of witness to which these varied readings also attest, has been a constant stimulus and inspiration to me and to so many others.

J. Robert Wright, D.Phil. (Oxon.), D.D., F.R. Hist. S.,
St. Mark's Professor of Ecclesiastical History
The General Theological Seminary
New York City

Notes

✠

1. With reference to the Calendar, those commemorated persons who are "Anglican" might be defined as 1) all who are members of the Church of England since the Reformation or of any other church now regarded as part of the Anglican Communion, or 2) all Christians hailing from England or from Britain since the beginnings there of Christianity who have not specifically renounced Anglican Church membership, as well as all who are members of any other church now regarded as part of the Anglican Communion, or 3) all Christians living anywhere who were members of the "undivided" church before the Reformation, as well as all since that time who are members of any church that is now regarded as part of the Anglican Communion.

The last of these definitions is obviously the broadest, and reflects the standard Anglican claim to be the continuation in England and in the Anglican Communion of the one undivided catholic church that existed everywhere from the beginning of Christianity up to the time of the Reformation. By this definition, for example, just as the Roman Catholic Church would not hesitate to claim Antony of Egypt as being "catholic" and hence one of its own because he was a Christian of that early period, so too he may be claimed by Anglicans or Episcopalians, since they too claim to be part of that same catholic church, properly understood. Further see J. Robert Wright, "Anglicanism, *Ecclesia Anglicana,* and Anglican: An Essay on Terminology," in *The Study of Anglicanism,* ed. Stephen Sykes and John Booty (London and Philadelphia, 1988), 424–429.

2. The best general discussion of this topic for the Church of England is Michael Perham, *The Communion of Saints* (Alcuin Club Collections no. 62, London, 1980). Earlier treatments that are still quite helpful include pp. 201–244 of *Liturgy and Worship,* ed. W.K. Lowther Clarke and Charles Harris (London, 1932), and *The Commemoration of Saints and Heroes of the*

Notes

Faith in the Anglican Communion (The Report of a Commission appointed by the Archbishop of Canterbury), London 1958. For the best standard one-volume reference work in English on the cult of saints in England from the beginnings to the Reformation, including all saints of English origin, all who were venerated in the calendar of the Sarum Rite in medieval England, all who appear in the calendar of the English Book of Common Prayer, all saints recorded in English place-names, and the most important representative saints of Ireland, Scotland, and Wales, together with tables of iconography, patronage, and places as well as a calendar, see David Hugh Farmer, *The Oxford Dictionary of Saints,* third ed. (Oxford and New York, 1992). Further, see also Frances Arnold-Forster, *Studies in Church Dedications or England's Patron Saints* (3 vols., London, 1899).

3. For the Lutheran Calendar, see Philip H. Pfatteicher, *Festivals and Commemorations: Handbook to the Calendar in Lutheran Book of Worship* (Minneapolis, 1980).

4. For the Episcopal Church in the U.S.A., the best treatment of this topic is O.C. Edwards Jr., *For All Those Saints* (Cincinnati, 1981), 72 pages. Much helpful information is also found in *Prayer Book Studies,* vols. IX, XII, XVI, and XIX. Further, see also [Anon.], *On the Dedications of American Churches,* "Compiled by Two Laymen of the Diocese of Rhode Island" (Cambridge Mass., 1891), 154 pages.

5. 1988 General Convention resolution A097a (page 639); 1991 General Convention resolution A119s. Cf. Thomas J. Talley, "The Passion of Witness: Prolegomena to the Revision of the Sanctoral Calendar," pp. 12–17 of *The Occasional Papers of the Standing Liturgical Commission,* Collection Number One, Occasional Paper Number Two (N.Y., 1987), esp. p. 16. Further "Guidelines and Procedures for Continuing Revision" are presently under consideration. For the earlier background, see *Prayer Book Studies IX* (N.Y., 1957), 24–28, 35–38, as well as occasional scattered references to criteria for the Episcopal Church in *Prayer Book Studies XII, XVI, and XIX.* For discussions of criteria followed in the Church of England, see Michael Perham, *op. cit.,* 127–141, and Clarke and Harris, *op. cit.,* 239–243.

Notes

6. For this process in the Roman Catholic Church, see Kenneth L. Woodward, *Making Saints* (N.Y., 1990), and Michael Freze, *The Making of Saints* (Huntington Indiana, 1991). Of the official total of 264 popes in the Roman Catholic Church, 78 have been canonized, and eight beatified.

7. For information pertinent to the Eastern Orthodox Churches, see *The Commemoration of Saints and Heroes of the Faith in the Anglican Communion, op. cit.,* ch. 4 ("The Recognition of Saints in the Eastern Orthodox Churches"); *The Byzantine Saint,* ed. Sergei Hackel (London, 1981), and Vladimir Demshuk, *Sainthood and Canonization.*

8. Cf. J. Robert Wright, "An Anglican Response to *The One Mediator, the Saints, and Mary*" (address given at the first symposium of The Center for Ecumenical Marian Studies, St. Mary's University, San Antonio, Texas, 8 July 1992; publication forthcoming). For the same tradition in the Church of England, see A.M. Allchin, "The Prayers of the Saints: Two Seventeenth-Century Views," in *Marian Library Studies* n.s. vol. 10 (December 1978), 131–145; and Michael Perham, *op. cit.,* 122–125. Further see John Macquarrie, *Mary for All Christians* (Grand Rapids, 1990).

The Episcopal Calendar of Lesser Feasts

✠

DECEMBER

1 Nicholas Ferrar, Deacon, 1637
2 Channing Moore Williams, Missionary
  Bishop in China and Japan, 1910
4 John of Damascus, Priest, c. 760
5 Clement of Alexandria, Priest, c. 210
6 Nicholas, Bishop of Myra, c. 342
7 Ambrose, Bishop of Milan, 397

JANUARY

10 William Laud, Archbishop of
   Canterbury, 1645
12 Aelred, Abbot of Rievaulx, 1167
13 Hilary, Bishop of Poitiers, 367
17 Antony, Abbot in Egypt, 356
19 Wulfstan, Bishop of Worcester, 1095
20 Fabian, Bishop and Martyr of Rome, 250
21 Agnes, Martyr at Rome, 304
22 Vincent, Deacon of Saragossa, and
   Martyr, 304
23 Phillips Brooks, Bishop of Massachusetts,
   1893
26 Timothy and Titus, Companions of Saint
   Paul

27 John Chrysostom, Bishop of
   Constantinople, 407
28 Thomas Aquinas, Priest and Friar, 1274

FEBRUARY

 1 Brigid (Bride), 523
 3 Anskar, Archbishop of Hamburg,
   Missionary to Denmark and Sweden,
   865
 4 Cornelius the Centurion
 5 The Martyrs of Japan, 1597
13 Absalom Jones, Priest, 1818
14 Cyril, Monk, and Methodius, Bishop,
   Missionaries to the Slavs, 869, 885
15 Thomas Bray, Priest and Missionary,
   1730
23 Polycarp, Bishop and Martyr of Smyrna,
   156
27 George Herbert, Priest, 1633

MARCH

 1 David, Bishop of Menevia, Wales, c. 544
 2 Chad, Bishop of Lichfield, 672
 3 John and Charles Wesley, Priests, 1791,
   1788
 7 Perpetua and her Companions, Martyrs
   at Carthage, 202
 9 Gregory, Bishop of Nyssa, c. 394
12 Gregory the Great, Bishop of Rome, 604
17 Patrick, Bishop and Missionary of
   Ireland, 461
18 Cyril, Bishop of Jerusalem, 386

20 Cuthbert, Bishop of Lindisfarne, 687
21 Thomas Ken, Bishop of Bath and Wells,
      1711
22 James De Koven, Priest, 1879
23 Gregory the Illuminator, Bishop and
      Missionary of Armenia, c. 332
27 Charles Henry Brent, Bishop of the
      Philippines, and of Western New York,
      1929
29 John Keble, Priest, 1866
31 John Donne, Priest, 1631

APRIL

1 Frederick Denison Maurice, Priest, 1872
2 James Lloyd Breck, Priest, 1876
3 Richard, Bishop of Chichester, 1253
4 Martin Luther King, Jr., Civil Rights
      Leader, 1968
8 William Augustus Muhlenberg, Priest,
      1877
9 William Law, Priest, 1761
11 George Augustus Selwyn, Bishop of New
      Zealand, and of Lichfield, 1878
19 Alphege, Archbishop of Canterbury, and
      Martyr, 1012
21 Anselm, Archbishop of Canterbury, 1109
29 Catherine of Siena, 1380

MAY

2 Athanasius, Bishop of Alexandria, 373
4 Monnica, Mother of Augustine of
      Hippo, 387

8 Dame Julian of Norwich, c. 1417
9 Gregory of Nazianzus, Bishop of
    Constantinople, 389
19 Dunstan, Archbishop of Canterbury, 988
20 Alcuin, Deacon, and Abbot of Tours,
    804
24 Jackson Kemper, First Missionary Bishop
    in the United States, 1870
25 Bede, the Venerable, Priest, and Monk of
    Jarrow, 735
26 Augustine, First Archbishop of
    Canterbury, 605

*The First Book of Common Prayer, 1549, is appropriately
observed on a weekday following the Day of Pentecost*

JUNE

1 Justin, Martyr at Rome, c. 167
2 The Martyrs of Lyons, 177
3 The Martyrs of Uganda, 1886
5 Boniface, Archbishop of Mainz,
    Missionary to Germany, and Martyr,
    754
9 Columba, Abbot of Iona, 597
10 Ephrem of Edessa, Syria, Deacon, 373
14 Basil the Great, Bishop of Caesarea, 379
15 Evelyn Underhill, 1941
16 Joseph Butler, Bishop of Durham, 1752
18 Bernard Mizeki, Catechist and Martyr in
    Rhodesia, 1896
22 Alban, First Martyr of Britain, c. 304
28 Irenaeus, Bishop of Lyons, c. 202

JULY

11 Benedict of Nursia, Abbot of Monte
   Cassino, c. 540
17 William White, Bishop of Pennsylvania,
   1836
24 Thomas a Kempis, Priest, 1471
26 The Parents of the Blessed Virgin Mary
27 William Reed Huntington, Priest, 1909
29 Mary and Martha of Bethany
30 William Wilberforce, 1833
31 Joseph of Arimathaea

AUGUST

 7 John Mason Neale, Priest, 1866
 8 Dominic, Priest and Friar, 1221
10 Laurence, Deacon, and Martyr at Rome,
   258
11 Clare, Abbess at Assisi, 1253
13 Jeremy Taylor, Bishop of Down, Connor,
   and Dromore, 1667
14 Jonathan Myrick Daniels, 1965
18 William Porcher DuBose, Priest, 1918
20 Bernard, Abbot of Clairvaux, 1153
25 Louis, King of France, 1270
27 Thomas Gallaudet, 1902 and Henry
   Winter Syle, 1890
28 Augustine, Bishop of Hippo, 430
31 Aidan, Bishop of Lindisfarne, 651

SEPTEMBER

 1 David Pendleton Oakerhater, Deacon
   and Missionary, 1931

2 The Martyrs of New Guinea, 1942
9 Constance, Nun, and her Companions,
   1878
12 John Henry Hobart, Bishop of New
   York, 1830
13 Cyprian, Bishop and Martyr of Carthage,
   258
16 Ninian, Bishop in Galloway, c. 430
18 Edward Bouverie Pusey, Priest, 1882
19 Theodore of Tarsus, Archbishop of
   Canterbury, 690
20 John Coleridge Patteson, Bishop of
   Melanesia, and his Companions,
   Martyrs, 1871
25 Sergius, Abbot of Holy Trinity, Moscow,
   1392
26 Lancelot Andrewes, Bishop of
   Winchester, 1626
30 Jerome, Priest, and Monk of Bethlehem,
   420

OCTOBER

1 Remigius, Bishop of Rheims, c. 530
4 Francis of Assisi, Friar, 1226
6 William Tyndale, Priest, 1536
9 Robert Grosseteste, Bishop of Lincoln,
   1253
14 Samuel Isaac Joseph Schereschewsky,
   Bishop of Shanghai, 1906
15 Teresa of Avila, Nun, 1582
16 Hugh Latimer and Nicholas Ridley,
   Bishops, 1555, and Thomas Cranmer,
   Archbishop of Canterbury, 1556

17 Ignatius, Bishop of Antioch, and Martyr,
     c. 115
19 Henry Martyn, Priest, and Missionary to
     India and Persia, 1812
26 Alfred the Great, King of the West
     Saxons, 899
29 James Hannington, Bishop of Eastern
     Equatorial Africa, and his
     Companions, Martyrs, 1885

NOVEMBER

 2 Commemoration of All Faithful
     Departed
 3 Richard Hooker, Priest, 1600
 7 Willibrord, Archbishop of Utrecht,
     Missionary to Frisia, 739
10 Leo the Great, Bishop of Rome, 461
11 Martin, Bishop of Tours, 397
12 Charles Simeon, Priest, 1836
14 Consecration of Samuel Seabury, First
     American Bishop, 1784
16 Margaret, Queen of Scotland, 1093
17 Hugh, Bishop of Lincoln, 1200
18 Hilda, Abbess of Whitby, 680
19 Elizabeth, Princess of Hungary, 1231
20 Edmund, King of East Anglia, 870
23 Clement, Bishop of Rome, c. 100
25 James Otis Sargent Huntington, Priest
     and Monk, 1935
28 Kamehameha and Emma, King and
     Queen of Hawaii, 1864, 1885

Thanksgiving Day is appropriately observed on the fourth
Thursday of November

Readings for the Lesser Feasts

✠

Nicholas Ferrar

Deacon, 1637

A reading from a Farewell Letter *written by Nicholas Ferrar to his parents on April 10, 1613, when he thought he was dying*

And you, my most dearest parents, if God shall take me from you now, I beseech you be of good comfort and be not grieved at my death, which I undoubtedly hope shall be to me the beginning of eternal happiness. And to you no loss, for you shall with inestimable joy receive me in the Kingdom of heaven to reign there with you and my dearest brother Erasmus and your other children that are departed in the Lord. If I go before you, you must come shortly after; think it is but a little forbearance of me. It was God that gave me to you, and if he take me from you be not only content but most joyful that I am delivered from this vale of misery and wretchedness. I know that through the infinite mercy of my gracious God it shall be my happiness, for I shall then, I know, enjoy perpetual quietness and peace and be delivered from those continual combats and temptations which afflict my poor soul. Oh Lord, thou knowest, I may truly say: "from my youth up, thy terrors have I suffered with a troubled mind." My soul hath been almost rent through violent temptations that have assaulted it, for to thy glory, oh Lord, will I confess my own weaknesses and the great dangers which thou hast delivered me from. It was the Lord that kept me, else had they devoured my soul and made it desolate. And this God that hath kept me ever since I was born, ever since I came out of your womb, my most dear mother, will preserve me to the end, I know, and give me grace that I shall live in his faith and die in his fear and favour, and rest in his peace, and rise in his power, and reign in his glory.

The Ferrar Papers, ed. Bernard Blackstone (Cambridge, 1938), 233–236 (spelling and punctuation modernized)

DECEMBER 2

✠

Channing Moore Williams
Missionary Bishop in China and Japan, 1910

A reading from a letter by Channing Moore Williams, Missionary Bishop in China and Japan, written from China on June 25, 1858

Melanchthon, in the ardor of his first love, thought it would be only necessary to tell sinners of the gracious Saviour he had found, and numbers would immediately flee unto Him, to hide them from the wrath of an offended God. But Luther replied, "Old Satan is too strong for young Melanchthon." This is a lesson it might be well for some to learn, who seem to think that so soon as the gospel is made known to the heathen, they will see it so infinitely superior to their own false and foolish systems—that it possesses such beauty, and such suitableness to their wants, they will forthwith close with its offers of mercy. But it is not to be expected that Satan will give up China thus easily. He considers it the fairest portion of his dominions. Here he rules with undisputed sway over the hearts of 360,000,000 people—a third of our race. Here he has entrenched himself for ages behind the most effectual barriers—not the least formidable of which is an overweening pride, and a system

4

of morality, second only to that taught in the Bible—the practice of which he persuades them is possible, and restores them to that state of holiness of heart, which they think all have at birth.

Now, the missionary who comes, and the Church which sends the missionary, must make up their minds, that there will be a long and desperate struggle before Satan is expelled. Every inch of ground will have to be contested. That he shall be driven from China none can doubt. The heathen have been given to the Son of God for His inheritance, and the uttermost parts of the earth for His possession. We should therefore labor and faint not. Because we do not meet with immediate success, we have no *right* to be discouraged, and relax our efforts. This is too much like dictating to God. It is almost as if we should say to Him: because you do not give success in the manner, the measure, and at the time we wish, we work no longer.

Appeal of the Foreign Committee of the Board of Missions of the Protestant Episcopal Church (N.Y., 10 November 1858), 8–9

DECEMBER 4

✠

John of Damascus
Priest, c. 760

A reading from the Exposition of the Orthodox Faith *by John of Damascus, Priest, written in the mid-eighth century*

By the cross all things have been made right. The power of God is the word of the cross, either because God's might, that is, the victory over death, has been revealed to us by it, or because, just as the four extremities of the cross are held fast and bound together by the bolt in the middle, so also by God's power the height and depth and length and breadth, that is, every creature visible and invisible, is maintained.

The cross was given to us as a sign on our forehead, just as the circumcision was given to Israel: for by it we believers are separated and distinguished from unbelievers. The cross is the shield and weapon against, and trophy over, the devil. "This is the seal that the destroyer may not touch you," says the Scripture. This is the resurrection of those lying in death, the support of those who stand, the staff of the weak, the rod of the flock, the safe-conduct of the earnest, the perfection of those that press forward, the salvation of soul and body, the aversion of all things evil, the patron of all things good, the abolition of sin, the ground of resurrection, the tree of eternal life.

So, then, this same truly precious and august tree, on which Christ offered himself as a sacrifice for our sakes, is to be venerated as sanctified by contact with his holy body and blood. Likewise the nails, the spear, the clothes, his sacred tabernacles which are the manger, the cave, Golgotha which brings salvation, the tomb which gives life, Sion, the chief stronghold of the churches and the like, are to be venerated. For if those things which we love and house and clothe are to be longed after, how much the rather should we long after that which belonged to God our Savior, by means of which we are in truth saved.

Moreover we venerate even the image of the precious and life-giving cross, although made of another tree, not honoring the tree (God forbid) but the image as a symbol of Christ.

It behoves us, then, to worship the sign of Christ. For wherever the sign may be, there also will he be. But it does not behove us to venerate the material of which the image of the cross is composed, even though it be gold or precious stones. Everything, therefore, that is dedicated to God we venerate, but conferring the worship on him.

The tree of life which was planted by God in Paradise prefigured this precious cross. For since by a tree was death, it was fitting also that life and resurrection should be bestowed by a tree.

The Fount of Knowledge 3, On the Orthodox Faith 4, 11: PG 94, 1129–1132

DECEMBER 5

✠

Clement of Alexandria
Priest, c. 210

A reading from a treatise On Spiritual Perfection *written by Clement of Alexandria, Priest, in the late second century*

Accordingly all our life is a festival. Being persuaded that God is everywhere present on all sides, we praise him as we till the ground, we sing hymns as we sail the sea, we feel his inspiration in all that we do.

Prayer is most fitting for those who have a right knowledge of the Divinity and that excellence of character which is agreeable to the Divinity, that is, for those who know what things are truly good, and what should be asked for, and when, and how. But it is the height of folly to ask of those who are not gods as if they were gods, or to ask what is inexpedient (that which is evil for oneself) under the impression that it is good. Since then the good God is one, we and the angels are right in praying that we may receive from God alone either the bestowal or continuance of good things. But we do not ask alike, for it is not the same thing to ask that the gift may be continued, and to strive to obtain it in the first instance. Prayer for the avoidance of evil is also a kind of prayer. But we must never employ a prayer of this kind for the injury of others.

Every place, then, and every time at which we entertain the thought of God is truly hallowed. Yet if we are at once right-minded and thankful when making our request in prayer, we contribute in a way to the granting of the petition, receiving with joy the desired object through the instrumentality of our prayers. For when the Giver of all good meets with readiness on our part, all good things follow at once on the mere conception in the mind. Certainly prayer is a test of the attitude of the character toward what is fitting. And if voice and speech are given to us with a view to understanding, how can God help hearing the soul and the mind by itself, inasmuch as soul already apprehends soul and mind apprehends mind?

Wherefore God has no need to learn various tongues, as human interpreters have, but understands at once the minds of all. Whatever our voice signifies to us, that is what our thought utters to God, since even before the creation God knew that it would come into our mind. It is permitted to us therefore to speed our prayer even without a voice, if we concentrate all our spiritual energy upon the inner voice of the mind by turning to God with full attention.

Stromata 7, 7.39, 43: PG 9, 456, 464

DECEMBER 6

✠

Nicholas

Bishop of Myra, c. 342

A reading of excerpts from the legendary biographies of Nicholas, Bishop of Myra in the mid-fourth century

When every land subject to Constantine's rule had received decrees of toleration, all Christians and confessors returned to their own states. Thus the citizens of Myra received back their pontiff Nicholas, an unbloodied victor though by nature and will a martyr. Strengthened by the gifts which God had granted him, he cured all the infirm from everywhere.

So famous and renowned did he quickly become not only among the faithful but among many of the infidels as well that in all peoples' minds he was admired beyond the power of words.

At the time when Constantine the First, who chose the true religion, was administering the Roman Empire, and the great pontiff Nicholas was training his people to accept righteous dogma and, if anything alien or weakening were to be found in it, to root it out and destroy it, at that time all the Orthodox people were gathered at Nicea to establish a true constitution of the faith and to drive away the blasphemous doctrine of Arius, with a view to peaceful reconciliation within the whole Church. This was brought about by the determination that the Son was equal in honor with the Father and that both persons were conjoint. The admirable Nicholas helped to effect this as a member of the sacred synod, and he strenuously resisted the casuistry of Arius, reducing to naught his every tenet. Then when the correct rule of faith had been transmitted to all, Nicholas left Nicea and returned to his own flock. There by precept and example he acutely and fervently set forth the doctrine of faith, leading all toward virtue.

Charles W. Jones. Saint Nicholas of Myra, Bari, and Manhattan (Chicago, 1978), 19, 63

DECEMBER 7

✠

Ambrose

Bishop of Milan, 397

A reading from a letter by Ambrose, Bishop of Milan, written in the later fourth century

The church's foundation is unshakable and firm against the assaults of the raging sea. Waves lash at the church but do not shatter it. Although the elements of this world constantly beat upon the church with crashing sounds, the church possesses the safest harbor of salvation for all in distress. Although the church is tossed about on the sea, it rides easily on rivers, especially those rivers that Scripture speaks of: "The rivers have lifted up their voice." These are the rivers flowing from the heart of the one who is given drink by Christ and who receives from the Spirit of God. When these rivers overflow with the grace of the Spirit, they lift up their voice.

There is also a stream which flows down on God's saints like a torrent. There is also a rushing river giving joy to the heart that is at peace and makes for peace. Whoever has received from the fullness of this river, like John the Evangelist, like Peter and Paul, lifts up the voice. Just as the apostles lifted up their voices and preached the Gospel throughout the world, so those who drink these waters begin to preach the good news of the Lord Jesus.

Drink, then, from Christ, so that your voice may also be heard. Store up in your mind the water that is Christ, the water that praises the Lord. Store up water from many sources, the water that rains down from the clouds of prophecy.

Whoever gathers water from the mountains or draws it from springs, is personally a source of dew like the clouds. Fill your soul, then, with this water, so that your land may not be dry, but watered by your own springs. Whoever reads much and understands much, receives fullness, and whoever is full refreshes others. Wherefore Scripture says: "If the clouds are full, they will pour rain on the earth."

Therefore let your words be rivers, clean and limpid. Solomon says: "The weapons of the understanding are the lips of the wise;" and in another place he says: "Let your lips be bound with wisdom." That is, let the meaning of your words shine forth, let understanding blaze out. See that your addresses and expositions do not need to invoke the authority of others, but let your words be their own defense. Let no word escape your lips in vain or be uttered without depth of meaning.

Letter 2, 1–2, 4–5, 7; PL 16 (edit. 1845), 879, 881

William Laud

Archbishop of Canterbury, 1645

A reading from the Epistle Dedicatory [to King Charles I] at the beginning of A Relation of the Conference between William Laud, Lord Archbishop of Canterbury, and Mr. Fisher the Jesuit, *published in 1639*

No one thing hath made conscientious men more wavering in their own minds, or more apt and easy to be drawn aside from the sincerity of religion professed in the Church of England, than the want of uniform and decent order in too many churches of the kingdom; and the Romanists have been apt to say: The houses of God could not be suffered to lie so nastily, as in some places they have done, were the true worship of God observed in them, or did the people think that such it were. It is true, the inward worship of the heart is the great service of God, and no service acceptable without it; but the external worship of God in His Church is the great witness to the world, that our heart stands right in that service of God. Take this away, or bring it into contempt, and what light is there left "to shine before men, that they may see our devotion, and glorify our Father which is in heaven?" And to deal clearly with your Majesty, these thoughts are they, and no other, which have made me labour so much as I have done for decency and an orderly settlement of the external worship of God in the Church; for of that which is inward there can be no witness among men, nor no example for men.

Now, no external action in the world can be uniform without some ceremonies; and these in religion, the ancienter they be the better, so they may fit time and place. Too many overburden the service of God, and too few leave it naked. And scarce anything hath hurt religion more in these broken times than an opinion in too many men, that because Rome had thrust some unnecessary and many superstitious ceremonies upon the Church, therefore the Reformation must have none at all; not considering therewhile, that ceremonies are the hedge that fence the substance of religion from all the indignities which profaneness and sacrilege too commonly put upon it. And a great weakness it is, not to see the strength which ceremonies, things weak enough in themselves, God knows,—add even to religion itself.

The Works of the Most Reverend Father in God, William Laud, D.D., Sometime Lord Archbishop of Canterbury, vol. 2 (L.A.C.T., Oxford 1849), xvi-xvii

JANUARY 12

✠

Aelred
Abbot of Rievaulx, 1167

A reading from the Mirror of Love *by Aelred, Abbot of Rievaulx, written in 1142–1143*

The perfection of love for others lies in the love of one's enemies. We can find no greater inspiration for this than grateful remembrance of the wonderful patience of Christ. He who is fairer than all the children of men offered his fair face to be spat upon by sinful humans; he allowed those eyes that rule the universe to be blind-folded by the wicked; he bared his back to the scourges; he submitted that head which strikes terror in principalities and powers to the sharpness of the thorns; he gave himself up to be mocked and reviled, and at the end he endured the cross, the nails, the lance, the gall, the vinegar, remaining always gentle, meek and full of peace.

In short, "he was led like a sheep to the slaughter, and like a lamb before the shearers he kept silent, and did not open his mouth."

Who could listen to that wonderful prayer, so full of warmth, of love, of unshakable serenity—"Father, forgive them"—and hesitate to embrace one's enemies with overflowing love? "Father," he says, "forgive them." Is any gentleness, any love, lacking in this prayer?

Yet he put into it something more. It was not enough to pray for them; he wanted also to make excuses for them. "Father, forgive them, for they do not know what they are doing." They are great sinners, yes, but they have little judgment; therefore, "Father, forgive them." They are nailing me to the cross, but they do not know who it is that they are nailing to the cross: "If they had known, they would never have crucified the Lord of glory"; therefore, "Father, forgive them." They think he is a lawbreaker, an impostor claiming to be God, a seducer of the people. I have hidden my face from them, and they do not recognize my glory; therefore, "Father, forgive them, for they do not know what they are doing."

If we wish to resist the promptings of our sinful nature, we must enlarge the whole horizon of our love to contemplate the loving gentleness of the humanity of the Lord. If we wish to savor the joy of such love with greater perfection and delight, we must extend even to our enemies the embrace of true love.

Mirror of Love 3, 5: PL 195, 582

✠

Hilary

Bishop of Poitiers, 367

A reading from the treatise On the Trinity *by Hilary, Bishop of Poitiers, written in the mid-fourth century*

I chanced upon the books which, according to the tradition of the Hebrew faith, were written by Moses and the prophets, and found in them words spoken by God the Creator testifying of himself: "I am that I am," and again, "He that is, has sent me unto you." I confess that I was amazed to find in them an indication concerning God so exact that it expressed in the terms best adapted to human understanding an unattainable insight into the mystery of the divine nature. For no property of God which the mind can grasp is more characteristic of God than existence, since existence, in the absolute sense, cannot be predicated of that which shall come to an end, or of that which has had a beginning, and he who now joins continuity of being with the possession of perfect felicity could not in the past, nor can in the future, be non-existent; for whatsoever is divine can neither be originated nor destroyed. Wherefore, since God's eternity is inseparable from himself, it was worthy of God to reveal this one thing, that "He is," as the assurance of his absolute eternity.

For according to the words spoken to Moses, "He who is, has sent me unto you," we obtain the unambiguous conception that absolute being belongs to God, since that which "is" cannot be thought of or spoken of as not being. For being and not being are contraries, nor can these mutually exclusive descriptions be simultaneously true of one and the same object; for while the one is present, the other must be absent. Therefore, where anything "is," neither conception nor language will admit of its not being. When our thoughts are turned backwards, and are continually carried back further and further to understand the nature of "him who is," this sole fact about him, that he is, remains ever prior to our thoughts; since that quality, which is infinitely present in God, always withdraws itself from the backward gaze of our thoughts, though they reach back to an infinite distance. The result is that the backward straining of our thoughts can never grasp anything prior to God's property of absolute existence; since nothing presents itself to enable us to understand the nature of God even though we go on seeking to eternity, save always the fact that God always is. That then which has both been declared about God by Moses, that of which our human intelligence can give no further explanation: that very quality the Gospels testify to be a property of God Only-begotten; since in the beginning was the Word, and since the Word was with God, and since he was the true Light, and since God Only-begotten is in the bosom of the Father, and since Jesus Christ is God over all.

Therefore he "was," and he "is," since he is from him who always is what he is. But to be from him, that is to say, to be from the Father, is birth. Moreover, to be always from him, who always is, is eternity; but this eternity is derived not from himself, but from the Eternal. And from the Eternal nothing can spring but what is eternal; for if the Offspring is not eternal, then neither is the Father, who is the source of generation, eternal. Now since it is the special characteristic of his being that his Father always exists, and that he is always his Son, and since eternity is expressed in the name "He that is," therefore, since he possesses absolute being, he possesses also eternal being.

On the Trinity 1, 5; 12, 24: PL 10, 28, 447–448

16

✠

Antony

Abbot in Egypt, 356

A reading from the Life of Antony *by Athanasius, Bishop of Alexandria, written c. 357 shortly after Antony's death*

When Antony was about eighteen or twenty years old, his parents died, leaving him with an only sister. He cared for her as she was very young, and also looked after their home.

Not six months after his parents' death, as he was on his way to church for his usual visit, he began to think of how the apostles had left everything and followed the Savior, and also of those mentioned in the book of Acts who had sold their possessions and brought the apostles the money for distribution to the needy. He reflected too on the great hope stored up in heaven for such as these. This was all in his mind when, entering the church just as the Gospel was being read, he heard the Lord's words to the rich man: "If you want to be perfect, go and sell all you have and give the money to the poor and you will have treasure in heaven. Then come and follow me."

It seemed to Antony that the words of the Gospel had been spoken directly to him. Immediately he left the church and gave away to the villagers all the property he had inherited, about 200 acres of very beautiful and fertile land, so that it would cause no distraction to his sister and himself. He sold all his other possessions as well, giving to the poor the considerable sum of money he collected.

The next time he went to church he heard the Lord say in the Gospel: "Do not be anxious about tomorrow." Without a moment's hesitation he went out and gave the poor all that he had left. He placed his sister in the care of some well-known and trustworthy virgins and arranged for her to be brought up in the convent. Then he gave himself up to the ascetic life, not far from his own home. He kept a careful watch over himself and practiced great austerity. He did do manual work because he had heard the words: "If anyone will not work, do not let him eat." He spent some of his earnings on bread and the rest he gave to the poor.

Having learned that we should always be praying, even when we are by ourselves, he prayed without ceasing. Indeed, he was so attentive when Scripture was read that nothing escaped him.

Seeing the kind of life he lived, the villagers and all the good people he knew called him the friend of God, and they loved him.

Life of Antony 2–4: PG 26, 842–846

JANUARY 19

✛

Wulfstan
Bishop of Worcester, 1095

A reading from an account of the oath of canonical obedience made by Wulfstan, Bishop of Worcester, to Lanfranc, Archbishop of Canterbury, c. 1070

This custom of holy religious observance prevails: when a bishop is consecrated he should reverently go to the metropolitan [of the province] and there make profession of obedience to the metropolitan; he should also leave a written profession of the same obedience to the metropolitan and his successors. But at the time when I, Wulfstan, was ordained bishop of the Hwiccas in the city of Worcester, Stigand had seized the holy church of Canterbury to which all my predecessors had been subject. By force and guile he had expelled the metropolitan from his see, and in contempt of the apostolic see he had rashly presumed to wear the pallium [or symbol of metropolitan rank] which he had seized. For this reason he was summoned, excommunicated and condemned by the Roman pontiffs Leo, Victor, Stephen, Nicholas, and Alexander. Nevertheless, in the hardness of his heart he persisted in his obduracy. During this time therefore orders were given throughout England by the popes forbidding anyone to reverence him as bishop; further, no one was to go to him for ordination. For this reason some bishops of the English at that time went for consecration to Rome, and others to France, while others again had recourse to their fellow-bishops at home. But I went to Aldred, bishop of the church of York, and I have put off making my profession of canonical obedience down to this day.

Now, therefore, I, a bishop, and according to the canons, offer to you, Lanfranc, metropolitan of the holy church of Canterbury, my profession of obedience to your orders and to those of your successors. And as God is my witness I promise to keep my pledge.

English Historical Documents 2, ed. David C. Douglas (London, 1968), 635–636

✠

Fabian

Bishop and Martyr of Rome, 250

A reading from the earliest account of a papal election, the choosing of Fabian as bishop of Rome in the year 236, as recorded in the Ecclesiastical History *of Eusebius, Bishop of Caesarea*

When the brethren had all assembled with the intention of electing a successor to the episcopate, and a large number of eminent and distinguished men were in the thoughts of many, Fabian, who was present, came into no one's mind. But suddenly, it is said, a dove fluttered down from above and settled upon his head, plainly following the example of the descent of the Holy Spirit upon the Savior in the form of a dove. At this, as if moved by one divine inspiration, with the utmost enthusiasm all the people with one soul cried out "he is worthy," and then and there they took him and set him upon the bishop's throne.

Ecclesiastical History 6, 29: Loeb ii, 80–83

JANUARY 21

✠

Agnes

Martyr at Rome, 304

A reading from the treatise On Virgins *by Ambrose, Bishop of Milan, at the account concerning Agnes, who was martyred at Rome in the early fourth century*

Today is the birthday of Saint Agnes, who is said to have suffered martyrdom at the age of twelve. The cruelty that did not spare her youth shows all the more clearly the power of faith in finding one so young to bear it witness.

There was little or no room in that small body for a wound. Though she could scarcely receive the blow, she could rise superior to it. Girls of her age cannot bear even their parents' frowns and, pricked by a needle, weep as for a serious wound. Yet she shows no fear of the blood-stained hands of her executioners. She stands undaunted by heavy, clanking chains. She offers her whole body to be put to the sword by fierce soldiers. She is too young to know of death, yet is ready to face it. Dragged against her will to the altars, she stretches out her hands to the Lord in the midst of the flames, making the triumphant sign of Christ the victor on the altars of sacrilege. She puts her neck and hands in iron chains, but no chain can hold fast her tiny limbs.

A new kind of martyrdom! Too young to be punished, yet old enough for a martyr's crown. Unfitted for the contest, yet effortless in victory, she shows herself masterful in valor despite the handicap of youth. In the midst of tears, she sheds no tears herself. The crowds marvel at her recklessness in throwing away her life untasted, as if she had already lived life to the full. All are amazed that one not yet of legal age can give her testimony to God. So she succeeds in convincing others of her testimony about God, though her testimony in human affairs could not yet be accepted. What is beyond the power of nature, they argue, must come from its creator.

What menaces there were from the executioner, to frighten her; what promises made, to win her over; what influential people desired her in marriage! She answered: "To hope that any other will please me does wrong to my Spouse. I will be his who first chose me for himself. Executioner, why do you delay? If eyes that I do not want can desire this body, then let it perish." She stood still, she prayed, she offered her neck. Agnes preserved her virginity, and gained a martyr's crown.

On Virgins 1.2, 5, 7–9: PL 16 (edit. 1845), 189–191

JANUARY 22

✠

Vincent

Deacon of Saragossa, and Martyr, 304

A reading from a sermon of Augustine, Bishop of Hippo, about Vincent, Deacon of Saragossa, who was martyred in the early fourth century

"To you has been granted on Christ's behalf not only that you should believe in him but also that you should suffer for him." Vincent had received both these gifts and held them as his own. He displayed his faith in what he said, his endurance in what he suffered.

We ought not to rely on our own feelings when we speak out, nor be confident in our own strength when we undergo temptation. For whenever we speak prudently as we should, our wisdom comes from Christ, and whenever we endure evils courageously, our long-suffering comes from him.

Vincent conquered in him who conquered the world. Christ said: "In this world you will suffer persecution," but in such wise that the persecution will not overwhelm, and the attack will not overcome you. Against Christ's army the world arrays a twofold battleline. It offers temptation to lead us astray; it strikes terror into us to break our spirit. Hence if our personal pleasures do not hold us captive, and if we are not frightened by brutality, then the world is overcome. At both of these approaches Christ rushes to our aid, and the Christian is not conquered. If you were to consider in Vincent's martyrdom only human endurance, then his act is unbelievable from the outset. But first recognize the power to be from God, and Vincent ceases to be a source of wonder.

Such savagery was being vented upon the martyr's body while such serenity issued from his lips, such harsh cruelties were being inflicted on his limbs while such assurance rang out in his words, that we should think that, by some miracle, as Vincent suffered, one person was speaking while another was being tortured. And this was true; another person was speaking. Christ in the Gospel promised this to those who were to be his witnesses, to those whom he was preparing for contests of this kind: "Do not give thought to how or what you are to speak. For it is not you who speak, but the Spirit of your Father who speaks within you." Thus it was Vincent's body that suffered, but the Spirit who spoke.

Sermon 276, 1–2: PL 38, 1256

JANUARY 23

✠

Phillips Brooks

Bishop of Massachusetts, 1893

A reading from the Lectures on Preaching *by Phillips Brooks, Bishop of Massachusetts, published in 1877*

Preaching is the bringing of truth through personality. It must have both elements.

This was the method by which Christ chose that His Gospel should be spread through the world. It was a method that might have been applied to the dissemination of any truth, but we can see why it was especially adapted to the truth of Christianity. For that truth is preëminently personal. However the Gospel may be capable of statement in dogmatic form, its truest statement we know is not in dogma but in personal life. Christianity is Christ; and we can easily understand how a truth which is of such peculiar character that a person can stand forth and say of it "I am the Truth," must always be best conveyed through, must indeed be almost incapable of being perfectly conveyed except through personality.

There are two aspects of the minister's work, which we are constantly meeting in the New Testament. They are really embodied in two words, one of which is "*message*," and the other is "*witness*." "This is the message which we have heard of Him and declare unto you," says St. John in his first Epistle. "We are his witnesses of these things," says St. Peter before the Council at Jerusalem. In these two words together, I think, we have the fundamental conception of the matter of all Christian preaching. It is to be a message given to us for transmission, but yet a message which we cannot transmit until it has entered into our own experience, and we can give our own testimony of its spiritual power. The minister who keeps the

24

word "message" always written before him, as he prepares his sermon in his study, or utters it from his pulpit, is saved from the tendency to wanton and wild speculation, and from the mere passion of originality. He who never forgets that word "witness," is saved from the unreality of repeating by rote mere forms of statement which he has learned as orthodox, but never realized as true. If you and I can always carry this double consciousness, that we are messengers, and that we are witnesses, we shall have in our preaching all the authority and independence of assured truth, and yet all the appeal and convincingness of personal belief.

[There] is an immense amount of preaching which must be called preaching about Christ as distinct from preaching Christ. There are many preachers who seem to do nothing else, always discussing Christianity as a problem instead of announcing Christianity as a message, and proclaiming Christ as a Saviour. I do not undervalue their discussions. But I think we ought always to feel that such discussions are not the type or ideal of preaching. They may be necessities of the time, but they are not the work which the great Apostolic preachers did, or which the true preacher will always most desire. Definers and defenders of the faith are always needed, but it is bad for a church, when its ministers count it their true work to define and defend the faith rather than to preach the Gospel. Beware of the tendency to preach about Christianity, and try to preach Christ. To discuss the relations of Christianity and Science, Christianity and Society, Christianity and Politics, is good. To set Christ forth to men so that they shall know Him, and in gratitude and love become His, that is far better.

These are the elements of preaching, then,—Truth and Personality. The truth is in itself a fixed and stable element; the personality is a varying and growing element. In the union of the two we have the provision for the combination of identity with variety, of stability with growth, in the preaching of the Gospel.

Lectures on Preaching: edit. Zondervan (Grand Rapids, c. 1950), 5, 7, 14–15, 20–21, 28

JANUARY 26

✠

Timothy and Titus
Companions of St. Paul

A reading from the account about Timothy and Titus, companions of St. Paul, in the Ecclesiastical History *of Eusebius, Bishop of Caesarea in the early fourth century*

By his preaching to the Gentiles Paul had laid the foundations of the churches from Jerusalem by a round-about route as far as Illyricum. This is obvious from his own words and from Luke's account in the Acts. Similarly, from Peter's language we can gather the names of the provinces in which he preached the gospel of Christ to the circumcised, proclaiming the message of the New Covenant. It is clearly stated in the epistle which, as I said, is accepted as his, in which he writes to the Hebrews of the Dispersion in Pontus and Galatia, Cappadocia, Asia, and Bithynia. But how many of them and which ones became genuine enthusiasts, and were judged fit to shepherd the churches founded by the apostles, is not easy to determine, except for those whose names can be extracted from the statements of Paul. For he had innumerable fellow-workers or—as he himself called them—fellow-soldiers. Most of these he has honored with an imperishable memory, paying them constant tribute in his own letters. Again, Luke in the Acts, in listing Paul's disciples, mentions them by name. We may instance Timothy, stated to have been the first bishop appointed to the see of Ephesus, as was Titus to the churches of Crete.

Ecclesiastical History 3, 4: PG 20, 219–220

JANUARY 27

✠

John Chrysostom
Bishop of Constantinople, 407

A reading from a homily of John Chrysostom, Bishop of Constantinople, who died in exile on September 14, 407

"Where two or three are gathered in my name, there am I in their midst." It is, indeed, proper to a great and strong friendship that it maintains unity among those who love one another. "Are there people so wretched," I hear you say, "that they do not desire to have Christ in their midst?"

There certainly are: we who fight one another. Perhaps you will object scornfully: "What are you saying? Don't you see that we are all within the same walls, within the same church, unanimous in the same fold, without the slightest dissension, crying in unison under the leadership of the same shepherd, listening together to what is said, and praying in common? And you talk about fights and discords!"

Yes, I speak about fights, and I am neither mad nor misled. I see what I see, and I know that we are in the same fold and under the same shepherd. And that is why I deplore so much more that in spite of all these signs of togetherness, we are divided. "But," you will say, "tell us what division there is among ourselves?" Here there is none, but as soon as your meeting is over, one starts criticizing another; one publicly harms another; one is devoured by envy, by avarice or cupidity; another practices violence; another abandons himself to sensuality; another yields to deceit or fraud. If your souls could be stripped naked, you would realize that I am right in all that I am saying and you would recognize that I am not mad.

27

You will say: "We are not doing that sort of thing to harm others but to protect ourselves." It is this precisely that grieves me: living among kindred, we feel it necessary to be on our guard lest some-one harm us, and we feel we must take so many precautions. The cause of all this is frequent lying and trickery, a great weakening of charity, and constant quarrels. Hence, there are a good number of people who have more trust in pagans than in Christians. Surely, this is a source of confusion, tears, and sighs.

Therefore, respect that Table in which we all participate. Re-spect Christ immolated for us. Respect the sacrifice that is offered. After participating in such a Table, and sharing such Food, why take up arms against one another when we should all together be armed against the devil? It is this which makes us weak. Far from gathering all our shields on one common front against the devil we unite to fight our own kindred; we line up under the devil's com-mand instead of fighting against him. Let us repeat: we aim our arrows at our own kindred. "What arrows?" you ask. The arrows of tongue and lips. Not only arrows and javelins cause wounds. Cer-tain words inflict even more profound wounds.

How can we put an end to this kind of war? By reflecting that a word pronounced against one's own is a poison shot from the mouth, and that calumnies affect a member of Christ. "But," you reply, "I have been insulted." If your neighbor has harmed you, ask God to show mercy. The neighbor is your kin, one of Christ's own members. The neighbor is called to the one same Table with you.

Homily 8 on Romans: PG 60, 464–466

✠

Thomas Aquinas
Priest and Friar, 1274

A reading from a work about the Eucharist by Thomas Aquinas, Priest and Friar, composed in 1264

Since it was the will of God's only-begotten Son that mortals should share in his divinity, he assumed our nature in order that by becoming human he might make us divine. Moreover, when he took our flesh he dedicated the whole of its substance to our salvation. He offered his body to God the Father on the altar of the cross as a sacrifice for our reconciliation. He shed his blood for our ransom and purification, so that we might be redeemed from our wretched state of bondage and cleansed from all sin. But to ensure that the memory of so great a gift would abide with us for ever, he left his body as food and his blood as drink for the faithful to consume in the form of bread and wine.

O precious and wonderful banquet, that brings us salvation and contains all sweetness! Could anything be of more intrinsic value? Under the old law it was the flesh of calves and goats that was offered, but here Christ himself, the true God, is set before us as our food. What could be more wonderful than this? No other sacrament has greater healing power; through it sins are purged away, virtues are increased, and the soul is enriched with an abundance of every spiritual gift. It is offered in the Church for the living and the dead, so that what was instituted for the salvation of all may be for the benefit of all. Yet, in the end, no one can fully express the sweetness of this sacrament, in which spiritual delight is tasted at its very source, and in which we renew the memory of that surpassing love for us which Christ revealed in his passion.

It was to impress the vastness of this love more firmly upon the hearts of the faithful that our Lord instituted this sacrament at the Last Supper. As he was on the point of departing this world to go to the Father, after celebrating the Passover with his disciples, he bequeathed it as a perpetual memorial of his passion. It was the fulfillment of ancient figures and the greatest of all his miracles, while for those who were to experience the sorrow of his departure, it was destined to be a unique and abiding consolation.

Opusculum 57, on the feast of Corpus Christi, 1–4

FEBRUARY 1

✠

Brigid (Bride)
523

A reading from the Topography of Ireland *by the historian Gerald of Wales concerning Brigid, Abbess of Kildare in the late fifth and early sixth centuries*

At Kildare, in Leinster, where the glorious Brigid is celebrated, many miracles deserve to be recorded, amongst which the fire of Saint Brigid comes first. This they call inextinguishable, not that it could not be extinguished, but because the sisters feed it with fuel and so carefully that it has ever continued burning from the time of the Virgin. Notwithstanding the great quantity of wood that has been consumed during so long a time, yet the ashes have never accumulated. When, in the time of Brigid, twenty nuns served their Lord there, she made the twentieth. After her glorious transit

30

nineteen always remained and the number was not increased. After each had kept the fire in order on her own night, on the twentieth night the last sister heaped wood on the fire, saying: "Brigid, keep your own fire, for the night has fallen to you," and the fire being left so was found still burning in the morning. The fire is surrounded by a circular fence of twigs within which no male may enter, and if one should chance to presume to enter, which was sometimes attempted by giddy persons, he escaped not, without enduring punishment. Also, it is permitted for only women to blow on the fire, and for these, not with their own breath, but only with bellows or fans.

Topography of Ireland 34–36: The Historical Works of Giraldus Cambrensis, ed. Thomas Wright (London, 1905), 96–97

FEBRUARY 3

✠

Anskar

Archbishop of Hamburg, Missionary to Denmark and Sweden, 865

A reading from the account concerning Anskar, Archbishop of Hamburg and Bremen in the mid-ninth century, from the History of the Archbishops of Hamburg-Bremen *by Adam of Bremen*

Since there could not readily be found a preacher who would go to the Danes because of their barbarous cruelty (on account of which everyone shuns those people) the blessed Anskar, inspired, as we believe, by the Holy Spirit and desirous of obtaining martyr-

31

dom in whatever way he could, of his own accord presented himself with his associate Autbert, as being ready to go not only among the barbarians but also both into prison and to death for Christ. And so they spent two years in the kingdom of the Danes and converted many of the heathen to the Christian faith. And when, on their return thence, the emperor asked them a second time to make trial of the grace of the Gospel with the remotest peoples, the Swedes, the dauntless champion of Christ, Anskar, gladly set out for Denmark, taking with him as preachers the brethren Gislemar and Witmar. Leaving Gislemar there with Harold, Anskar himself and Witmar sailed across to Sweden where they were kindly received by King Björn and were permitted publicly to preach the Word of God. And so in the course of one year they won many to the Lord Jesus Christ.

The emperor and his great nobles then felicitated Saint Anskar on the deliverance of the heathen and rendered great thanks to Christ. In a general council of clerics which he held, the pious ruler, desirous of fulfilling his parent's will, appointed Hamburg, the city of the Transalbingians, as the metropolitan see for all the barbarous nations of the Danes, the Swedes, and likewise the Slavs and the other peoples living round about. And he had Anskar consecrated as first archbishop of this see.

History of the Archbishops of Hamburg-Bremen by Adam of Bremen, xv (17)–xvi (18), transl. Francis J. Tschan (N.Y., 1959), 22–23.

FEBRUARY 4

✠

Cornelius the Centurion

A reading about Cornelius the Centurion from the Ecclesiastical History *of Eusebius, Bishop of Caesarea in the early fourth century*

Thus with the powerful cooperation of heaven the whole world was suddenly lit by the sunshine of the saving word. At once, in accordance with the Holy Scriptures, the voice of its inspired evangelists and apostles went forth into all the earth, and their words to the ends of the world. In every town and village, like a well-filled threshing-floor, churches shot up bursting with eager members. People who through the error they had inherited from generations of ancestors were in the grip of the old spiritual sickness of idol-worship, by the power of Christ and through the teaching of his followers and the miracles they wrought were freed, as it were, from cruel masters and found release from galling fetters. They turned their backs on devilish polytheism in all its forms, and acknowledged that there was one God only, the fashioner of all things. Him they honored with the ordinances of true religion through that divine, reasonable worship of which our Savior sowed the seed in the life of humankind.

The divine grace was now being poured on the other nations too. First, at Palestinian Caesarea Cornelius with his entire household, through divine revelation and the agency of Peter, embraced the Christian faith. He was followed by many other Gentiles at Antioch, who had heard the preaching of those dispersed by the persecution of Stephen's time. The Antioch church was now flourishing and growing rapidly, and a large number of the prophets from Jerusalem were there, accompanied by Barnabas and Paul and another group of brethren as well. It was at that time and in that city that the name of Christian first appeared, as if from a copious and life-giving fountain.

Ecclesiastical History 2, 3: PG 20, 141–144

FEBRUARY 5

✠

The Martyrs of Japan
1597

A reading from a contemporary account of the death of the Jesuit brother Paul Miki and his companions, first martyrs of Japan, crucified and killed at Nagasaki on February 5, 1597

The crosses were set in place. Father Pasio and Father Rodriguez took turns encouraging the victims. Their steadfast behavior was wonderful to see. The Father Bursar stood motionless, his eyes turned heavenward. Brother Martin gave thanks to God's goodness by singing psalms. Again and again he repeated: "Into your hands, Lord, I entrust my life." Brother Francis Branco also thanked God in a loud voice. Brother Gonsalvo in a very loud voice kept saying the Our Father and Hail Mary.

Our brother, Paul Miki, saw himself standing now in the noblest pulpit he had ever filled. To his "congregation" he began by proclaiming himself a Japanese and a Jesuit. He was dying for the Gospel he preached. He gave thanks to God for this wonderful blessing and he ended his "sermon" with these words: "As I come to this supreme moment of my life, I am sure none of you would suppose I want to deceive you. And so I tell you plainly: there is no way to be saved except the Christian way. My religion teaches me to pardon my enemies and all who have offended me. I do gladly pardon the Emperor and all who have sought my death. I beg them to seek baptism and be Christians themselves."

Then he looked at his comrades and began to encourage them in their final struggle. Joy glowed in all their faces, and in Louis' most of all. When a Christian in the crowd cried out to him that he would soon be in heaven, his hands, his whole body, strained upward with such joy that every eye was fixed on him.

Anthony, hanging at Louis' side, looked toward heaven and called upon the holy names—"Jesus, Mary!" He began to sing a psalm: "Praise the Lord, you children!" (He learned it in catechism class in Nagasaki. They take care there to teach the children some psalms to help them learn their catechism.)

Others kept repeating "Jesus, Mary!" Their faces were serene. Some of them even took to urging the people standing by to live worthy Christian lives. In these and other ways they showed their readiness to die.

Then, according to Japanese custom, the four executioners began to unsheathe their spears. At this dreadful sight, all the Christians cried out, "Jesus, Mary!" And the storm of anguished weeping then rose to batter the very skies. The executioners killed them one by one. One thrust of the spear, then a second blow. It was over in a very short time.

Chapter 14, 109–110: Acta Sanctorum, February, 1, 769

FEBRUARY 13

✠

Absalom Jones
Priest, 1818

A reading from the sermon preached in St. Thomas Church, Phila-delphia, by Absalom Jones, Priest, on January 1, 1808, in thanks-giving for the abolition of the African slave trade

The history of the world shows us, that the deliverance of the children of Israel from their bondage, is not the only instance in which it has pleased God to appear in behalf of oppressed and distressed nations, as the deliverer of the innocent, and of those who call upon his name. He is as unchangeable in his nature and character, as he is in his wisdom and power. The great and blessed event, which we have this day met to celebrate, is a striking proof that the God of heaven and earth is the *same, yesterday, and to-day, and for ever.* Yes, my brethren, the nations from which most of us have descended, and the country in which some of us were born, have been visited by the tender mercy of the Common Father of the human race. He has seen the affliction of our countrymen, with an eye of pity. He has seen the wicked arts, by which wars have been fomented among the different tribes of the Africans, in order to procure captives, for the purpose of selling them for slaves. He has seen ships fitted out from different ports in Europe and America, and freighted with trinkets to be exchanged for the bodies and souls of men. He has seen the anguish which has taken place, when parents have been torn from their children, and children from their parents, and conveyed, with their hands and feet bound in fetters, on board of ships prepared to receive them. He has seen them thrust in crowds into the holds of those ships, where many of them have perished from want of air. He has seen such of them as

36

have escaped from that noxious place of confinement, leap into the ocean, with a faint hope of swimming back to their native shore, or a determination to seek an early retreat from their impending misery, in a watery grave. He has seen them exposed for sale, like horses and cattle, upon the wharves; or, like bales of goods, in warehouses of West Indian and American sea ports. He has seen the pangs of separation between members of the same family. He has seen them driven into the sugar, the rice, and the tobacco fields, and compelled to work—in spite of the habits of ease which they derived from the natural fertility of their own country in the open air, beneath a burning sun, with scarcely as much clothing upon them as modesty required. He has seen them faint beneath the pressure of their labours. He has seen them return to their smoky huts in the evening, with nothing to satisfy their hunger but a scanty allowance of roots, and these, cultivated for themselves, on that day only, which God ordained as a day of rest for man and beast. He has seen the neglect with which their masters have treated their immortal souls; not only in withholding religious instruction from them but, in some instances, depriving them of access to the means of obtaining it. He has seen all the different modes of torture, by means of the ship, the screw, the pincers, and the red-hot iron, which have been executed upon their bodies by inhuman overseers.

Inhuman wretches! though you have been deaf to their cries and shrieks, they have been heard in Heaven. The ears of Jehovah have been constantly open to them; he has heard the prayers that have ascended from the hearts of his people, and he has, as in the case of his ancient and chosen people the Jews, *come down to deliver* our suffering countrymen from the hands of their oppressors. He *came down* into the United States, when they declared, in the constitution which they framed in 1788, that the trade in our African fellow-men would cease in the year 1808; *he came down* into the British Parliament when they passed a law to put an end to the same iniquitous trade in May, 1807; *he came down* into the Con-

37

gress of the United States, the last winter, when they passed a similar law, the operation of which commences on this happy day. Dear land of our ancestors! thou shalt no more be stained with the blood of thy children, shed by British and American hands; the ocean shall no more afford a refuge to their bodies, from impending slavery; nor shall the shores of the British West India island, and of the United States, any more witness the anguish of families, parted forever by a public sale. For this signal interposition of the God of mercies, in behalf of our brethren, it becomes us this day to offer up our united thanks.

Black Gospel/White Church, ed. John M. Burgess (N.Y., 1982), 3–5

FEBRUARY 14

✠

Cyril, Monk, and Methodius, Bishop
Missionaries to the Slavs, 869, 885

A reading from an Old Slavonic Life of Cyril, Monk, and missionary to the Slavs in the ninth century

[Cyril,] already burdened by many hardships, became ill. At one point during his extended illness, he experienced a vision of God and began to sing this verse: "My spirit rejoiced and my heart exulted because they told me we shall go into the house of the Lord."

Afterward he remained dressed in the vestments that were to be venerated later, and rejoiced for an entire day, saying: "From now on, I am not the servant of the emperor or of any person on earth, but of almighty God alone. Before, I was dead; now I am alive and I shall live for ever. Amen."

The following day, he assumed the monastic habit and took the religious name Cyril. He lived the life of a monk for fifty days.

When the time came for him to set out from this world to the peace of his heavenly homeland, he prayed to God with his hands outstretched and his eyes filled with tears: "O Lord, my God, you have created the choirs of angels and spiritual powers; you have stretched forth the heavens and established the earth, creating all that exists from nothing. You hear those who obey your will and keep your commands in holy fear. Hear my prayer and protect your faithful people, for you have established me as their unsuitable and unworthy servant.

"Keep them free from harm and the worldly cunning of those who blaspheme you. Build up your church and gather all into unity. Make your people known for the unity and profession of their faith. Inspire the hearts of your people with your word and your teaching. You called us to preach the Gospel of your Christ and to encourage them to lives and works pleasing to you.

"I now return to you, your people, your gift to me. Direct them with your powerful right hand, and protect them under the shadow of your wings. May all praise and glorify your name, the Father, Son and Holy Spirit. Amen."

Once he had exchanged the gift of peace with everyone, he said: "Blessed be God, who did not hand us over to our invisible enemy, but freed us from his snare and delivered us from perdition." He then fell asleep in the Lord at the age of forty-two.

Chapter 18: Denkschriften der kaiserliche Akademie der Wissenschaften 19 (Vienna, 1870), 246

FEBRUARY 15

✠

Thomas Bray

Priest and Missionary, 1730

A reading from the original petition of Thomas Bray, Priest and Missionary, dated 1701, that resulted in the founding of the Society for the Propagation of the Gospel in that year

To the King's Most Excellent Majesty, the humble Petition of Thomas Bray, D. D., humbly sheweth, that the numbers of the inhabitants of your Majesty's provinces in America have of late years greatly increased; that in many of the colonies thereof, more especially on the continent, they are in very much want of instruction in the Christian religion, and in some of them utterly destitute of the same, they not being able to raise a sufficient maintenance for an orthodox clergy to live amongst them, and to make such other provision, as shall be necessary for the Propagation of the Gospel in those Parts.

Your petitioner further sheweth, that upon his late arrival into England from thence, and his making known the aforesaid matters in this city and kingdom, he hath great reason to believe, that many persons would contribute, as well by legacy, as gift, if there were any body corporate, and of perpetual succession now in being, and established in this kingdom, proper for the lodging of the said legacies and grants therein.

Now forasmuch as Your Majesty hath already been graciously pleased to take the state of the souls of Your Majesty's subjects in those Parts, so far into consideration, as to found, and endow a royal college in Virginia, [the College of William and Mary] for the religious education of their youth, your petitioner is thereby the more encouraged to hope, that Your Majesty will also favour any the like designs and ends, which shall be prosecuted by proper and effectual means.

Your petitioner therefore, who has lately been among Your Majesty's subjects aforesaid, and has seen their wants and knows their desires, is the more emboldened, humbly to request, that Your Majesty would be graciously pleased to issue letters patent, to such persons as Your Majesty shall think fit, thereby constituting them a body politick and corporate, and to grant them and their successors, such powers, privileges, and immunities as Your Majesty in great wisdom shall think meet and necessary for the effecting the aforesaid ends and designs.

John Wolfe Lydekker. Thomas Bray, 1658–1730, Founder of Missionary Enterprise (Church Historical Society Publication no. 14, Philadelphia, 1943), 23–24 (capitalization and spelling modernized)

FEBRUARY 23

✠

Polycarp
Bishop and Martyr of Smyrna, 156

A reading from the Martyrdom of Polycarp, *Bishop of Smyrna, who was burned alive and then stabbed to death on 23 February in the year 156*

The proconsul pressed Polycarp insistently: "Swear the oath, and I shall release you. Curse Christ." Polycarp answered: "Eighty-six years have I served him, and he did me no wrong. How can I blaspheme my king who saved me?" The proconsul persevered saying: "Swear by the fortune of Caesar." Polycarp answered: "If you vainly imagine that I shall swear by the fortune of Caesar, as you say, and pretend you do not know who I am, listen plainly: I am a Christian."

When the fire was ready, Polycarp took off all his clothes and loosened his under-garment. Immediately he was surrounded by the material for the burning. When they tried to fasten him also with nails, he said: "Leave me as I am. The One who gives me strength to endure the fire will also give me strength to stay quite still on the pyre, even without the precaution of your nails." So they bound him without nailing him. Thus bound with hands behind his back, he stood like a noble ram, chosen out for sacrifice from a great flock, a burnt offering ready and acceptable to God.

Looking up to heaven, he said: "Lord God Almighty, Father of your beloved and blessed Son Jesus Christ, through whom we have received full knowledge of yourself, God of angels and powers and all creation, of all the race of the righteous who live in your presence, I bless you for judging me worthy of this day and hour, so that in the company of the martyrs I may share the cup of your Christ, and so rise again to eternal life in soul and body, immortal through the power of the Holy Spirit. May I be received among the martyrs in your presence today as a rich and pleasing sacrifice. God of truth without any falsehood, you have prepared this and revealed it to me and now you have fulfilled your promise. For this and for everything I praise you, I bless you, I glorify you through the eternal high priest of heaven, Jesus Christ, your beloved Son. Through him be glory to you, together with him and the Holy Spirit, now and for ever. Amen."

When he had said "Amen" and finished the prayer, the officials at the pyre lit it. But, when a great flame burst out, those of us privileged to see it witnessed a strange and wonderful thing. Indeed, we have been spared in order to tell the story to others. Like a ship's sail swelling in the wind, the flame became a sort of arch forming a wall around the martyr's body. Surrounded by the fire, his body was like bread that is baking, or like gold and silver refined in a furnace, not like burning flesh. So sweet a fragrance came to us that it was like that of burning incense or some other precious spice.

But the evil one who is the enemy of the race of the righteous, seeing the greatness of Polycarp's witness and the blamelessness of his life from the beginning, and that he was crowned with the wreath of immortality and had won an incontestable prize, contrived it so that we should not recover his body although many were eager to do so and to touch his holy flesh.

They knew not that we can never abandon Christ who suffered for the salvation of those who are being saved throughout the whole world, the sinless one for sinners, nor can we worship any other. For we adore Christ as Son of God, but the martyrs we love as disciples and imitators of the Lord, and rightly because of their unsurpassable devotion to their own King and Master. May it also be our lot to be their companions and fellow disciples!

And so the centurion set Polycarp's body in the midst and burned it. So we later took up his bones, more precious than costly stones and more valuable than gold, and laid them away in a suitable place. There the Lord will permit us, so far as possible, to gather and celebrate with great gladness and joy the day of his martyrdom as a birthday, in memory of those who have fought the good fight before us and for the training and preparation of those who are to come hereafter.

Martyrdom of Polycarp 9, 3–18, 1: Musurillo, 8–17

FEBRUARY 27

✠

George Herbert

Priest, 1633

A reading from the poem called Aaron, *a reflection on Exodus 28 and the Christian Priesthood by George Herbert, Priest, published in 1633*

Holinesse on the head,
Light and perfections on the breast,
Harmonious bells below, raising the dead
To lead them unto life and rest.
Thus are true Aarons drest.

Profanenesse in my head,
Defects and darkness in my breast,
A noise of passions ringing me for dead
Unto a place where is no rest.
Poore priest thus am I drest.

Only another head
I have, another heart and breast,
Another musick, making live not dead,
Without whom I could have no rest:
In him I am well drest.

Christ is my only head,
My alone only heart and breast,
My only musick, striking me ev'n dead;
That to the old man I may rest,
And be in him new drest.

So holy in my head,
Perfect and light in my deare breast,
My doctrine tun'd by Christ, (who is not dead,
But lives in me while I do rest)
Come people; Aaron's drest.

"Aaron," from The Temple: the Church

MARCH 1

✠

David

Bishop of Menevia, Wales, c. 544

A reading from the Life of David, *Bishop of Menevia in the mid-sixth century and patron saint of Wales, by Rhygyfarch the Wise, written c. 1090*

When the third day of the week was come, at cock crowing, the monastery was filled with angelic choirs, and was melodious with heavenly songs, and was full of sweetest fragrance. At the hour of matins, when the clerks were replying to the songs with psalms and hymns, the Lord Jesus deigned to bestow his presence for consolation, as he had promised by the angel. When David saw him, he altogether rejoiced in spirit. "Take me after you," he said. With these words he gave back his life to God, Christ being his companion, and accompanied by the angelic host he went to the abodes of heaven.

Who then could bear the weeping of the saints, the sad sighs of the anchorites, the groaning of the priests, the wailings of the

disciples who exclaimed, "By whom shall we be taught?", the grief
of the pilgrims who said, "By whom shall we be aided?", the de-
spair of kings who said, "By whom shall we be appointed, corrected
and established? Who will be so very mild as David? Who shall
intercede for us to the Lord?" And who could then bear the lamen-
tations of peoples, the grief of paupers, the cryings of sick folk, the
clamor of monks, the tears of virgins, of married people, penitents,
young men, young women, boys, girls, of infants sucking breasts?
The voice of all was the voice of mourners, for kings grieved for
him as an arbiter, the old wailed for him as one of them, adults
honored him, and indeed he was one whom all persons venerated
as if God.

And so his body, carried in the arms of holy brethren, and
accompanied by a great throng, was honorably committed to the
earth and buried in his own monastery. But his soul without any
limit of passing time was crowned for ever and ever.

May David, whose festival we devoutly celebrate on earth, unite
us by his intercessions to the angelic citizens, God being over all.

Life of St. David, transl. A.W. Wade-Evans (N.Y., 1923), 30–31

MARCH 2

✠

Chad

Bishop of Lichfield, 672

*A reading about Chad, Bishop of Lichfield in the seventh century,
from the* Ecclesiastical History of England *by Bede the Venerable, Priest and Monk of Jarrow*

46

A holy man, modest in his ways, learned in the Scriptures, and careful to practice all that he found in them: This was a priest named Chad, a brother of the most reverend Bishop Cedd, and at that time Abbot of Lastingham.

When he became bishop, Chad immediately devoted himself to maintaining the truth and purity of the church, and set himself to practice humility and continence and to study. After the example of the Apostles, he traveled on foot and not on horseback when he went to preach the Gospel, whether in towns or country, in cottages, villages, or strongholds; for he was one of Aidan's disciples and always sought to instruct his people by the same methods as Aidan and his own brother Cedd.

Ecclesiastical History 3, 28: Colgrave and Mynors, 316–317

MARCH 3

✣

John and Charles Wesley
Priests, 1791, 1788

A reading from The Scripture Way of Salvation *by John Wesley, Priest, published in 1765*

The end is, in one word, salvation; the means to attain it, faith.

It is easily discerned, that these two little words, I mean faith and salvation, include the substance of all the Bible, the marrow, as it were, of the whole Scripture.

Let us then seriously inquire, What is salvation? What is that faith whereby we are saved? And, How are we saved by it?

And, first, let us inquire, What is salvation? The salvation which is here spoken of, is not what is frequently understood by that word, the going to heaven, eternal happiness. It is not a blessing which lies on the other side death; or, as we usually speak, in the other world. The very words of the text itself put this beyond all question: *"ye are saved."* It is not something at a distance; it is a present thing; a blessing which, through the free mercy of God, ye are now in possession of. Nay, the words may be rendered, and that with equal propriety, "Ye *have been* saved": So that the salvation which is here spoken of might be extended to the entire work of God, from the first dawning of grace in the soul, till it is consummated in glory.

But we are at present concerned only with that salvation which the apostle is directly speaking of. And this consists of two general parts, justification and sanctification.

Justification is another word for pardon. It is the forgiveness of all our sins; and, what is necessarily implied therein, our acceptance with God. The price whereby this hath been procured for us (commonly termed the meritorious cause of our justification), is the blood and righteousness of Christ; or, to express it a little more clearly, all that Christ hath done and suffered for us, till he "poured out his soul for the transgressors."

And at the same time that we are justified, yea, in that very moment, sanctification begins. In that instant we are born again, born from above, born of the Spirit: there is a *real* as well as a *relative* change.

From the time of our being born again the gradual work of sanctification takes place. We are enabled, "by the Spirit," to "mortify the deeds of the body," of our evil nature; and as we are more and more dead to sin, we are more and more alive to God. We go on from grace to grace, while we are careful to "abstain from all appearance of evil," and are "zealous of good works," as we have opportunity of doing good to all men; while we walk in all his ordinances blameless, therein worshipping him in spirit and in truth; while we take up our cross, and deny ourselves every pleasure that does not lead us to God.

But what is that faith through which we are saved? This is the second point to be considered.

Faith in general is defined by the apostle: *an evidence,* a divine *evidence and conviction* [the word means both] *of things not seen;* not visible, not perceivable either by sight, or by any other of the external senses.

Taking the word in a more particular sense, faith is a divine *evidence* and *conviction,* not only that "God was in Christ, reconciling the world unto himself," but also that Christ loved *me,* and gave himself for *me.* It is by this faith that we *receive Christ;* that we receive him in all his offices, as our Prophet, Priest, and King.

And, how are we justified by faith? In what sense is this to be understood? I answer, faith is the condition, and the only condition of justification. It is the *condition:* none is justified but he that believes: without faith no man is justified. And it is the *only condition:* this alone is sufficient for justification. Every one that believes is justified, whatever else he has or has not. In other words: no man is justified till he believes; every man, when he believes, is justified.

The Works of the Rev. John Wesley, A.M. (Third American complete and standard ed., N.Y., 1831); J.H. Leith. Creeds of the Churches (N.Y., 1963), 360–366

✠

Perpetua and her Companions
Martyrs at Carthage, 202

A reading from the Passion of Perpetua and her Companions, *who were martyred in the amphitheatre at Carthage on 7 March in the year 202*

On the day before we were to fight, I saw in a vision Pomponius the deacon come hither to the door of the prison and knock loudly. And I went out to him, and opened to him. Now he was clad in a white robe without a girdle, wearing shoes curiously wrought. And he said to me: "Perpetua, we are waiting for you; come." And he took hold of my hand, and we began to pass through rough and broken country. Painfully and panting did we arrive at last at an amphitheater, and he led me into the middle of the arena. And he said to me: "Fear not: I am here with you, and I suffer with you." And he departed. And I saw a huge crowd watching eagerly. Because I knew that I was condemned to the beasts, I marvelled that there were no beasts let loose on me. There came out an Egyptian, foul of look, with his attendants to fight against me.

We came near to one another and began to use our fists. My adversary wished to catch hold of my feet, but I kept on striking his face with my heels. I was lifted up into the air, and began to strike him in such fashion as would one that no longer trod on earth. But when I saw that the fight lagged, I joined my two hands, linking the fingers of the one with the fingers of the other. I caught hold of his head and he fell on his face, and I trod upon his head. The people began to shout, and my supporters to sing psalms. And I came forward to the trainer, and received the bough. He kissed me, and said to me: "Peace be with you, my daughter." And I began to go in triumph to the Gate of Life. And I awoke. And I perceived that

I should not fight with beasts but with the devil: but I knew the victory to be mine. Such were my doings up to the day before the games.

[*Such was the vision of Perpetua, and the account of her death follows:*]

The day of victory dawned, and they proceeded from the prison to the amphitheater, as if they were on their way to heaven. For the young women the devil made ready a mad heifer, an unusual animal selected for this reason, that he wished to match their sex with that of the beast. So after being stripped and enclosed in nets they were brought into the arena. The people were horrified, beholding in the one net a tender girl, in the other a woman fresh from child-birth, with milk dripping from her breasts. So they were recalled and dressed in tunics without girdles. Perpetua was tossed first, and fell on her loins. Sitting down she drew back her torn tunic from her side to cover her thighs, more mindful of her modesty than of her suffering. Then having asked for a pin she further fastened her disordered hair. For it was not seemly that a martyr should suffer with her hair dishevelled, lest she should seem to mourn in the hour of her glory. Then she rose, and seeing that Felicity was bruised, she approached and gave a hand to her, and lifted her up. The two stood side by side, and the cruelty of the people being now appeased, they were recalled to the Gate of Life.

The people asked for them to be brought into the open, that, when the sword pierced their bodies, these might lend their eyes for partners in the murder. They rose unbidden and made their way whither the people willed, after first kissing one another, that they might perfect their martyrdom with the rite of the Pax. Perpetua, that she might taste something of the pain, was struck on the bone and cried out, and she herself guided to her throat the wavering hand of the young untried gladiator. Perhaps so great a woman, who was feared by the unclean spirit, could not otherwise be slain unless she was willing.

Martyrdom 10, 18, 20–21: Musurillo, 116–131

Gregory
Bishop of Nyssa, c. 394

A reading from the Life of Moses *written in the late fourth century by Gregory, Bishop of Nyssa*

The vision of God is not achieved by sight and hearing nor is it acquired by any of the ordinary processes of mental apprehension. "For the eye has not seen, nor has the ear heard," nor does it belong to those things that usually enter the human heart. Anyone who would approach the knowledge of things sublime must first purify their manner of life from all sensual and irrational influences. Such a person must wash every preconceived opinion from the mind and withdraw from normal intercourse with one's spouse, that is, from sense perceptions that are, as it were, wedded to our nature. Thus purified, one may attempt to climb the mountain.

The contemplation of divine things, this mountain, is steep and difficult to climb, and the majority of people hardly ever reach even its foot. But if one were a Moses, one would ascend higher and hear the sound of trumpets which, as the biblical account says, becomes louder as one advances.

The multitudes were not capable of hearing the voice from above but relied on Moses to learn by himself the secrets and to teach the people whatever doctrine he might learn through instruction from above. This is also true of our arrangement in the church. Not everyone inclines toward apprehension of the mysteries, but, choosing from among themselves someone who is able to grasp things divine, they listen gratefully to that person, considering as trustworthy whatever they happen to hear from someone thus steeped in the divine mysteries.

What is the significance of the fact that Moses entered the darkness and then saw God in it? At first this account of the vision of God seems to contradict the earlier one, for, whereas then the Divine was seen in light, now the Divine is seen in darkness. But we should not regard this as inconsistent at the level of spiritual contemplation. Scripture by this teaches that in the initial stages religious knowledge comes as illumination. Therefore what is perceived to be contrary to religion is darkness, and escape from that darkness is achieved by participation in the light. But as the mind progresses from there, leaving behind everything that is observed, not only what sense comprehends but also what the intelligence thinks it sees, the mind presses on with its interior journey until by its persistent search for understanding it penetrates the invisible and incomprehensible, and there it sees God. Herein lies the true knowledge of the goal of our search: this is the seeing that consists precisely in not seeing, because the goal of our search transcends all knowledge, being surrounded on all sides by a wall of incomprehensibility as by a kind of darkness. And this is why John, the sublime one, who himself penetrated this illuminated darkness, writes that "No one has seen God at any time." By such a negative statement he is asserting that knowledge of the divine essence is inaccessible not only to humans but also to every created intelligence.

So it was that when Moses had progressed in the knowledge of God he claimed to see God in darkness, that is, he had come to know that in essence the deity is beyond all knowledge and comprehension. The text says: "Moses approached the dark cloud where God was." What God? The God who "made darkness his hiding place," as the Psalm says. For Scripture forbids that the Divine be likened to any of the things known by humans, since every concept which comes from some incomprehensible image by an approximate understanding and by guessing at the divine essence constitutes only an image of God and does not proclaim God. This then is truly the vision of God: never to be satisfied in the desire to see him.

Life of Moses 2, 157–165, 239: PG 44, 327–430

MARCH 12

✠

Gregory the Great
Bishop of Rome, 604

A reading from the treatise On Pastoral Care *written c. 591 by Gregory the Great, Bishop of Rome*

No one ventures to teach any art unless it has been learned after deep thought. With what rashness, then, would the pastoral office be undertaken by the unfit, seeing that the governing of souls is the art of arts! For who does not realize that the wounds of the mind are more hidden than the internal wounds of the body? Yet, although those who have no knowledge of the powers of drugs shrink from giving themselves out as physicians of the flesh, people who are utterly ignorant of spiritual precepts are often not afraid of professing themselves to be physicians of the heart. Likewise, although, by divine ordinance, those now in the highest positions are disposed to show a regard for religion, some there are who aspire to glory and esteem by an outward show of authority within the holy church. They crave to appear as teachers and covet ascendancy over others, and, as the Truth attests: "They seek the first salutations in the market place, the first places at feasts, and the first chairs in the synagogues."

These persons are all the less able to administer worthily what they have undertaken, the office of pastoral care, in that they have attained to the tutorship of humility by vanity alone. Obviously, in this tutorship, the tongue purveys mere jargon when one thing is learned and its contrary is taught.

Further, there are some who investigate spiritual precepts with shrewd diligence, but in the life they live they trample on what they have penetrated by their understanding. They hasten to teach what they have learned, not by practice, but by study, and belie in their conduct what they teach by words.

The conduct of a pastor should so far surpass the conduct of the people as the life of a shepherd sets one apart from the flock. For one who is so regarded that the people are called the flock, must carefully consider how necessary it is to maintain a life of rectitude. It is necessary, therefore, that such a person should be pure in thought, exemplary in conduct, discreet in keeping silence, profitable in speech, in sympathy a near neighbor to everyone, in contemplation exalted above all others, a humble companion to those who lead good lives, unbending in zeal for righteousness against the vices of sinners. Such a one must not be distracted from care for the inner life by preoccupation with the external, nor in solicitude for what is internal fail to give attention to the external.

Pastors should be exemplary in conduct, that by their manner of living they may show the way of life to those who are put under them, and so that the flock, following the teaching and conduct of the shepherd, may proceed the better through example rather than words. For one who by exigency of position must propose the highest ideals is bound by that same exigency to give a demonstration of those ideals. The voice of such a one penetrates the hearts of the hearers more readily, if the way of life commends what is being said. That which is enjoined in words will be helped to execution by example. Wherefore, it is said by the prophet: "Get you up upon a high mountain, you who bring good tidings to Sion."

Often, however, pastors by the very fact of their preeminence over others become conceited; and because everything is at their service, because their orders are quickly executed to suit their wishes, because all their subjects praise them for what they have done well but have no authority to criticize what they have done amiss and because they usually praise even what they ought to blame, the pastors' minds, led astray by those below, are lifted above themselves. While the pastors are outwardly surrounded by abounding favors, the truth within them is made void. Forgetful of who they are, they are diverted by the commendations of others, and believe themselves to be such as they hear themselves outwardly proclaimed to be, not such as they should inwardly judge themselves to be.

Treatise on Pastoral Care 1, 1–2; 2, 1, 3, 6: PL 77, 14–15, 25–28, 35

MARCH 17

✠

Patrick
Bishop and Missionary of Ireland, 461

A reading from the Confession *written in the mid-fifth century by Patrick, Bishop and Missionary of Ireland*

I, Patrick, a sinner, quite uncultivated and the least of all the faithful and utterly despicable to many, had as my father the deacon Calpornius, son of the late Potitus, a priest, who belonged to the town of Bannavem Taburniae. He had a small estate nearby, and it was there that I was taken captive. I was then about sixteen years old. I did not know the true God and I was taken into captivity in Ireland with so many thousands. We deserved this, because we drew away from God and did not keep his commandments and did not obey our priests who kept reminding us of our salvation. The Lord brought on us the fury of his anger and scattered us among many peoples even to the ends of the earth, where now I in my insignificance find myself among foreigners.

I came to the Irish peoples to preach the Gospel and endure the taunts of unbelievers, putting up with reproaches about my earthly pilgrimage, suffering many persecutions, even bondage, and losing my birthright of freedom for the benefit of others.

If I am worthy, I am ready also to give up my life, without hesitation and most willingly, for his name. I want to spend myself in that country, even in death, if the Lord should grant me this favor. I am deeply in his debt, for he gave me the great grace that through me many peoples should be reborn in God and then made perfect by confirmation, and everywhere among them clergy ordained for a people so recently coming to believe: one people gathered by the Lord "from the ends of the earth." As God had prophesied of old through the prophets: "The nations shall come to you from the ends of the earth." In another prophecy he said: "I have set you as a light among the nations, to bring salvation to the ends of the earth."

It is among that people that I want to "wait for the promise" made by God, who assuredly never tells a lie.

Confession 1, 15–16: PL 53, 808–809

✠

Cyril

Bishop of Jerusalem, 386

A reading from the Procatechesis *of Cyril, Bishop of Jerusalem, composed in the mid-fourth century*

Already, dear candidates for enlightenment, there is upon you the scent of blessedness. Already you are gathering spiritual flowers, with which to weave heavenly crowns. Already the fragrance of the Holy Spirit is refreshing you. Already you are at the entrance hall of the royal mansion; may the King lead you in.

What great dignity Jesus bestows upon you. You used to be called catechumens, which means having something drummed into your ears, hearing about the Christian hope yet not understanding it, hearing about the mysteries yet not perceiving them, hearing the Scriptures yet not sounding their depths. Now you no longer hear with your ears, but within your heart, for the indwelling Spirit is making your mind into a house of God. Henceforth, when you hear texts of Scripture concerning the mysteries, you will understand the things you did not know.

This charge I also give you. Study the things that are told you, and keep them for ever. Do not confuse them with ordinary homilies, which are indeed excellent and trustworthy but if neglected today may be attended to tomorrow. On the contrary, today's teaching on baptismal regeneration, if it be neglected, when can it be made up?

Now when the instruction is over, if any catechumen should ask what the teachers have said, reveal nothing to a stranger, for it is a divine secret we have delivered to you, even the hope of the life to come.

You who have been enrolled have become the sons and daughters of one Mother. When you arrive before the exorcisms are due to begin, let each of you speak only what helps to promote devotion, and if any of your number are not present, go and search for them.

May God at length show you that night whose darkness is daylight, that night of which it is said "The darkness shall not be dark unto you, and the night shall be light as the day." Then may the gate of paradise be opened to every man and woman among you, then may you enjoy the fragrant Christ-bearing waters. Then may you receive the name of Christian, and the power of things divine!

Procatechesis 1, 6, 11–13, 15: Cross, 1, 4, 6–10, 40, 43–44, 46–50

MARCH 20

✠

Cuthbert
Bishop of Lindisfarne, 687

A reading about Cuthbert, Bishop of Lindisfarne in the seventh century, from the Ecclesiastical History of England *by Bede the Venerable, Priest and Monk of Jarrow*

In the year of his death, King Egfrid appointed as bishop of Lindisfarne the holy and venerable Cuthbert, who for many years had lived a solitary life in great self-mastery of mind and body on a tiny island known as Farne, which lies in the ocean about nine miles from the church.

Thus Cuthbert served God in solitude for many years in a hut surrounded by an embankment so high that he could see nothing but the heavens for which he longed so ardently. Then it came about that a great synod was held under the presidency of Archbishop Theodore of blessed memory, and in the presence of King Egfrid. It assembled near the river Alne at a place called Twyford, or the Two Fords; and the whole company unanimously elected Cuthbert as bishop of the church of Lindisfarne.

As bishop he followed the example of the blessed Apostles and enhanced his dignity by his holy actions, protecting the people entrusted to him by his constant prayer and inspiring them to heavenly things by his salutary teachings. Like a good teacher, he taught others to do only what he first practiced himself. Above all else, he was afire with heavenly love, unassumingly patient, devoted to unceasing prayer, and kindly to all who came to him for comfort. He regarded as equivalent to prayer the labor of helping the weaker members with advice, remembering that he who said: "Thou shalt love the Lord thy God," also said: "Love thy neighbor." His self-discipline and fasting were exceptional, and through the grace of contrition he was always intent on the things of heaven. Lastly, whenever he offered the sacrifice of the Saving Victim to God, he offered his prayers to God not in a loud voice but with tears welling up from the depths of his heart.

When he had spent two years in his bishopric, Cuthbert returned to his island hermitage, God having made known to him that the day of his death was drawing near, or rather, the day of his entry into that life which alone may be called life.

Ecclesiastical History 4, 27–28: Colgrave and Mynors, 430–439

MARCH 21

✠

Thomas Ken

Bishop of Bath and Wells, 1711

A reading from An Exposition on the Church Catechism *by Thomas Ken, Bishop of Bath and Wells, published in 1685*

I believe, O blessed and adorable Mediator, that the Church is a society of persons, founded by Thy love to sinners, united into one body, of which Thou art the head, initiated by baptism, nourished by the eucharist, governed by pastors commissioned by Thee, and endowed with the power of the keys, professing the doctrine taught by Thee, and delivered to the saints, and devoted to praise and to love Thee.

I believe, O holy Jesus, that Thy Church is holy, like Thee its Author; holy, by the original design of its institution; holy, by baptismal dedication; holy, in all its administrations, which tend to produce holiness: and though there will be always a mixture of good and bad in it in this world, yet it has always many real saints in it; and therefore, all love, all glory, be to Thee.

I believe, Lord, this Church to be catholic or universal, made up of the collection of all particular churches; I believe it to be catholic in respect of time, comprehending all ages to the world's end, to which it is to endure; catholic in respect of all places, out of which believers are to be gathered; catholic in respect of all saving faith, of which this creed contains the substance, which shall in it always be taught; catholic in respect of all graces, which shall in it be practised; and catholic in respect of that catholic war it is to wage against all its ghostly enemies, for which it is called militant. O preserve me always a true member of Thy catholic Church, that I may always inseparably adhere to Thee, that I may always devoutly praise and love Thee.

Glory be to Thee, O Lord my God, who has made me a member of the particular Church of England, whose faith and government, and worship, are holy, and catholic, and apostolic, and free from the extremes of irreverence or superstition; and which I firmly believe to be a sound part of Thy Church universal, and which teaches me charity to those who dissent from me; and therefore all love, all glory, be to Thee.

O my God, give me grace to continue steadfast in her bosom, to improve all those helps to true piety, all those means of grace, all those incentives of Thy love, Thou has mercifully indulged me in her communion, that I may, with primitive affections and fervour, praise and love Thee.

London 1686, pp. 26–27; rpt. The Practice of Divine Love (N.Y., 1849), 30–31

MARCH 22

✠

James DeKoven
Priest, 1879

A reading from a letter of James DeKoven, Priest, dated 19 January 1872

To state briefly the view I myself have been taught:

I believe that in the Eucharist after the consecration of the elements, by the power of the Holy Ghost, the very Body and Blood of CHRIST, not by transubstantiation, consubstantiation, or any other device of human reason, but supernaturally, spiritually and ineffably, are present in the elements. I believe them to be present by the wonderful sacramental union which unites the outward sign to the thing signified.

I believe that because CHRIST's Body and Blood are there, CHRIST Himself is there; yet, because His Person is Divine, not so as to be confined to the elements.

I believe that, as the Patriarchs worshipped the SON OF GOD, appearing unto them under the form of an Angel; as the Jews worshipped that Presence of GOD which dwelt between the Cherubim; as our LORD's Humanity as subsisting in His Divine Person when here on earth, was adorable; as His sacrificed Body hanging on the Cross, and laid in the grave, because not separate from His Divine Person was adorable: so CHRIST, present in the elements, is also to be worshipped.

I believe that the Body and Blood of CHRIST, really and truly, but supernaturally and spiritually, present, are offered and pleaded before GOD by the Priest, for "a continual remembrance of CHRIST's death and passion, until His coming again."

I believe that CHRIST's Body and Blood, present in the elements, are offered to all who come to the Holy Altar. I believe that they are either mystically withdrawn from the unfaithful recipient, or that they are received by him to his condemnation. I believe that the faithful recipient does indeed become a partaker of CHRIST. He is made one with CHRIST, and CHRIST one with him. He dwells in CHRIST, and CHRIST in him.

The Holy Eucharist: A Correspondence, p. 14; Letter of 19 January 1872 to the Rev. James Craik of Louisville, Ky.

MARCH 23

✠

Gregory the Illuminator
Bishop and Missionary of Armenia, c. 332

A reading from The Teaching of St. Gregory, *"Apostle of Armenia" in the early fourth century, contained within the* History of the Armenians *by the historian Agathangelos*

[It was] at the time when the Lord called Moses in the midst of the fire and cloud to the top of the mountain of Sinai, and the vision of the glory of the Lord was burning like fire, when Moses took the commandments of the laws from the hands of God, and saw God was beneficent from his answer to him: "I am merciful and compassionate." Then he received the tradition of the authority of the priesthood, kingship, and prophecy from God. Then God gave him a type of the anointing of Christ, that first might occur examples and then the truth might come: He who is. Then God ordered him to make the horn of anointing and the thurible of incense.

The horn was the type of the anointing of Christ, and the thurible the type of the holy Virgin Mary. For as the former was full of the odor of sanctity, so also the Virgin was full of the Holy Spirit and the power of the Highest. The horn of oil was the type of the anointing of Christ, for those who were anointed once in his example were anointed from it. Thence also Aaron was anointed to the priesthood of the Lord, and he took the crown of priesthood, to anoint according to the same type, to place on them the veil, to serve the holiness of the Lord, and to order the daily bread on the table, which bore the type of the flesh of the Son of God.

Then Moses made the silver horn of his anointing from which were anointed the priests, prophets, and kings. Thence proceeded in order the unction in succession according to the command of the authority of the commandment, which proceeded in order by seniority. The mystery was preserved in the seed of Abraham, because they passed on the tradition to each other until John—priest, prophet, and baptist. And coming to him, it remained on him as on an heir. For it came to him from the first forefathers, the kings, prophets, and anointed priests, as to a keeper of tradition. And he gave the priesthood, the anointing, the prophecy, and the kingship to our Lord Jesus Christ.

And the apostles became the foundations, and received the grace of priesthood and prophecy and apostleship and knowledge of the heavenly mystery which came in the seed of Abraham, which John, the keeper of the tradition of the inheritance, gave to the Lord, and the Lord gave to the apostles. And he gave the keys of the kingdom into their hands, for the Son of God himself was the gate for those who enter. Concerning this the prophet declared: "This is the gate of the Lord, and the just enter through it." So John gave the priesthood and the power and the prophecy and the kingship to our Savior Christ, and Christ gave them to the apostles, and the apostles to the children of the church.

The Teaching of St. Gregory 431–433, 468: transl. Robert W. Thomson (Harvard Armenian Texts and Studies, 3; Cambridge, 1970), 95–96, 106

MARCH 27

✠

Charles Henry Brent
Bishop of the Philippines, and of Western New York, 1929

A reading of various remarks on Christian unity from Charles Henry Brent, Bishop of the Philippines and then of Western New York, who died in 1929

The unity of Christendom is not a luxury but a necessity. The world will go limping until Christ's prayer that all may be one is answered. We must have unity, not at all costs, but at all risks. A unified Church is the only offering we dare present to the coming Christ, for in it alone will He find room to dwell.

Do not be deceived; without unity the conversion of great nations is well-nigh hopeless. The success of missions is inextricably bound up with unity. It would seem that missionary progress in the future will depend mainly upon the Church's unity, and that national conversions can be brought about by no other influence.

It may be that up to the present a divided Church has been used by God for the extension of His Kingdom among men, but we have no guarantee that He will continue to do so. Indeed there are indications that the divided Church has passed the zenith of such power as it has had, and is declining toward desolation. Divided Christendom has had fair trial—it is a failure.

If it is a prophecy that the gates of hell shall not prevail against the Church, it is also prophecy that the Church divided against herself will fall. Disorder in the Church is more terrible than feuds in the family or civil war in the State. If war is an evil in national life, it is a thousandfold greater evil in Church life.

If unity has slipped from our grasp, it is the common fault of the Christian world. If it is to be regained it must be by the concerted action of all Christians. Every section has shared in shattering unity. Every section must share in the effort to restore it.

Is the Church to lead in unity? If so, she must begin by unifying herself. It is laughable to think of a warring Church preaching about a world at peace. There is no lesson which the Churches are learning of greater importance than the impotence of our divided Christianity. It is absurd to aim at a united mankind, or even a united Christian civilization, and to be content with a divided Church. A confused Church will be a potent factor in maintaining a confused world.

Things that Matter: The Best of the Writings of Bishop Brent, ed. Frederick Ward Kates (N.Y., 1949), 38–40

MARCH 29

✠

John Keble
Priest, 1866

A reading of excerpts from the Assize Sermon *preached on Sunday, July 14, 1833 by John Keble, Priest, and published under the title of* National Apostasy

What are the symptoms by which one may judge most fairly, whether or no a nation, as such, is becoming alienated from God and Christ?

And what are the particular duties of sincere Christians whose lot is cast by divine providence in a time of such dire calamity?

The case is at least possible, of a nation, having for centuries acknowledged, as an essential part of its theory of government, that, as a Christian nation, she is also a part of Christ's Church, and bound, in all her legislation and policy, by the fundamental rules of that Church—the case is, I say, conceivable, of a government and people, so constituted, deliberately throwing off the restraint, which in many respects such a principle would impose on them, nay, disavowing the principle itself; and that on the plea that other states, as flourishing or more so in regard of wealth and dominion, do well enough without it.

Under the guise of charity and toleration we are come almost to this pass, that no difference, in matters of faith, is to disqualify for our approbation and confidence, whether in public or domestic life. Can we conceal it from ourselves, that every year the practice is becoming more common, of trusting men unreservedly in the most delicate and important matters, without one serious inquiry, whether they do not hold principles which make it impossible for them to be loyal to their Creator, Redeemer, and Sanctifier?

The surest way to uphold or restore our endangered Church will be for each of her anxious children, in his own place and station, to resign himself more thoroughly to his God and Saviour in those duties, public and private, which are not immediately affected by the emergencies of the moment: the daily and hourly duties, I mean, of piety, purity, charity, justice. It will be a consolation understood by every thoughtful churchman, that, let his occupation be apparently never so remote from such great interests, it is in his power, by doing all as a Christian, to credit and advance the cause he has most at heart; and what is more, to draw down God's blessing upon it.

These cautions being duly observed, I do not see how any person can devote himself too entirely to the cause of the apostolical Church in these realms. There may be, as far as he knows, but a very few to sympathize with him. He may have to wait long, and very likely pass out of this world before he see any abatement in the triumph of disorder and irreligion. But if he be consistent, he possesses, to the utmost, the personal consolation of a good Christian: and as a true churchman, he has that encouragement which no other cause in the world can impart in the same degree—he is calmly, soberly, demonstrably, SURE, that, sooner or later, HIS WILL BE THE WINNING SIDE, and that the victory will be complete, universal, eternal.

The Oxford Movement, ed. Eugene R. Fairweather (N.Y., 1964), 39–47

MARCH 31

✠

John Donne
Priest, 1631

A reading from the meditation For Whom the Bell Tolls *by John Donne, Priest, composed in 1623 and published in 1624*

Perchance he for whom this bell tolls may be so ill, as that he knows not it tolls for him; and perchance I may think myself so much better than I am, as that they who are about me, and see my state, may have caused it to toll for me, and I know not that. The church is Catholic, universal, so are all her actions; all that she does belongs to all. When she baptizes a child, that action concerns me; for that child is thereby connected to that body which is my head too, and ingrafted into that body whereof I am a member. And when she buries a man, that action concerns me: all mankind is of one author, and is one volume; when one man dies, one chapter is not torn out of the book, but translated into a better language; and every chapter must be so translated; God employs several translators; some pieces are translated by age, some by sickness, some by war, some by justice; but God's hand is in every translation, and his hand shall bind up all our scattered leaves again for that library where every book shall lie open to one another.

As therefore the bell that rings to a sermon calls not upon the preacher only, but upon the congregation to come, so this bell calls us all; but how much more me, who am brought so near the door by this sickness. There was a contention as far as a suit (in which both piety and dignity, religion and estimation, were mingled), which of the religious orders should ring to prayers first in the morning; and it was determined, that they should ring first that rose earliest. If we understand aright the dignity of this bell that tolls for our evening prayer, we would be glad to make it ours by rising early, in that application, that it might be ours as well as his, whose indeed it is. The bell doth toll for him that thinks it doth; and though it intermit again, yet from that minute that that occasion wrought upon him, he is united to God. Who casts not up his eye to the sun when it rises? but who takes off his eye from a comet when that breaks out? Who bends not his ear to any bell which upon any occasion rings? but who can remove it from that bell which is passing a piece of himself out of this world? No man is an island, entire of itself; every man is a piece of the continent, a part of the main. If a clod be washed away by the sea, Europe is the less, as well as if a promontory were, as well as if a manor of thy friend's or of thine own were: any man's death diminishes me, because I am involved in mankind, and therefore never send to know for whom the bell tolls; it tolls for thee.

Devotions upon Emergent Occasions 18: edit. Paulist, 271–272

APRIL 1

✠

Frederick Denison Maurice
Priest, 1872

A reading from a sermon on the Lord's Prayer by Frederick Denison Maurice, Priest, preached in 1848

The Paternoster is not, as some fancy, the easiest, most natural, of all devout utterances. It may be committed to memory quickly, but it is slowly learnt by heart. Men may repeat it over ten times in an hour, but to use it when it is most needed, to know what it means, to believe it, yea, not to contradict it in the very act of praying it, not to construct our prayers upon a model the most unlike it possible, this is hard.

At certain periods in the history of the Church, especially when some reformation was at hand, men have exhibited a weariness of their ordinary theological teaching. It seemed to them that they needed something less common, more refined than that which they possessed. As the light broke in upon them, they perceived that they needed what was less refined, more common. The Creed, the Ten Commandments, the Lord's Prayer were found to contain the treasures for which they were seeking. The signs of such a period are surely to be seen in our day. We can scarcely think that we require reformation less than our fathers. I believe, if we are to obtain it, we too must turn to these simple documents; we must inquire whether there is not a wisdom hidden in them which we do not meet with elsewhere; whether they cannot interpret the dream of our lives better than all the soothsayers whom we have consulted about it hitherto.

Our: Much of the practical difficulty of the prayer lies assuredly in the first word of it. How can we look round upon the people

whom we habitually feel to be separated from us by almost impass-
able barriers; who are above us so that we cannot reach them, or
so far beneath us that the slightest recognition of them is an act of
gracious condescension; upon the people of an opposite faction to
our own, whom we denounce as utterly evil; upon men whom we
have reason to despise; upon the actual wrong-doers of society,
those who have made themselves vile, and are helping to make it
vile—and then teach ourselves to think that in the very highest
exercise of our lives these are associated with us. That when we
pray, we are praying for them and with them; that we cannot speak
for ourselves without speaking for them; that if we do not carry
their sins to the throne of God's grace, we do not carry our own;
that all the good we hope to obtain there belongs to them just as
much as to us, and that our claim to it is sure of being rejected if
it is not one which is valid for them also? Yet all this is included in
the word "Our."

Think how many causes are at work every hour of our lives to
make this opening word of the prayer a nullity and a falsehood.
How many petty disagreements are there between friends and
kinsfolk, people dwelling in the same house—so petty that there is
no fear of giving way to them, and yet great enough to cause
bitterness and estrangement, great enough to make this "Our
Father" a contradiction.

But when we say "Father," are we more in earnest? Do we mean
that He whom we call upon is a Father actually, not in some
imaginary metaphorical sense?

Our Father: There lies the expression of that fixed eternal relation which Christ's birth and death have established between the
littleness of the creature and the Majesty of the Creator; the one
great practical answer to the philosopher who would make heaven
clear by making it cold; would assert the dignity of the Divine
Essence by emptying it of its love and reducing it into nothingness.
Our Father, *which art in Heaven:* there lies the answer to all the
miserable substitutes for faith by which the invisible has been

lowered to the visible; which have insulted the understanding and cheated the heart; which have made united worship impossible because that can only be when there is One Being, eternal, immortal, invisible, to whom all may look up together, into whose presence a way is opened for all.

We know there is One who is willing to teach us how to pray this prayer in spirit and in truth; we know that there is One who is praying it. He who died for us and for all mankind, He who is ascended into Heaven, He who is true and in whom is no lie, did when He was here clothed with our mortality, does now in his glorified humanity say, in the full meaning of the words, for us and for his whole family above and below, "Our Father which art in Heaven."

Sermons on the Prayer Book and the Lord's Prayer, edit. London 1902, 283–293

APRIL 2

✠

James Lloyd Breck
Priest, 1876

A reading from two letters of James Lloyd Breck, Priest, written in April and December of 1842

Our dear Bishop has authorized us to purchase land and build a small house, and this we have accordingly done. We have purchased a tract of 460 acres of land on the Nashotah lakes, ten miles from Prairie Village, and yet more central to our Mission. *Nashotah* means *Two Lakes* (it is the Indian name for *twin* lakes), and these are so called from their resemblance to each other.

The students boarding with us are all theological, that is, those whom we intend for the Ministry. They are chiefly young men, sons of the farmers, and all communicants of the Church, save one that is too young, but is otherwise a Christian lad, who does a good deal of our *housework.* Our students, like ourselves, are *poor,* but not the less worthy for that. They seek the Ministry, but are unable to attain unto it without aid; and what aid can we give? We have a house; for this we pay no rent,—it belongs to the Church, and so do we. We have land; that is in like case; it is fertile beyond all calculation (that is to an Eastern man). They work four hours a day for their board and washing—and we give them their education without cost. Thus their clothing is their only expense; and to enable them to purchase this, we shall give them *six weeks* vacation during harvest, when they can earn the highest wages. In the winter they can split rails, for fencing in the spring. Our other students, not lay brethren of our House, will board with families nigh at hand, and pay for their tuition.

Brother Adams and myself work four hours, except when we are teaching or doing Missionary labor. We must all work for our board. This is the only way in which they will feel it their duty to labor and to study, and the only way in which our people will feel their duty to the Church, and to ourselves as the clergy of the same.

We rise at 5 A.M. Matins at 6. The Morning Service of the Church at 9. On Wednesdays and Fridays, the Litany at 12. On Thursdays the Holy Eucharist at the same hour of 12. The Evening Service of the Church at 3, and Family Prayer or Vespers at 6:30 or 7 P.M. Our students labor between 7 and 9 in the morning, and 1 and 3 in the afternoon.

Now that we are in a house of our own and the people see our readiness to undergo things unpleasant in themselves, they are made ready to bestow a portion of their produce on us.

The Life of the Reverend James Lloyd Breck, D.D., chiefly from Letters written by Himself, ed. Charles Breck (Third ed., N.Y., 1882/1886), 29, 33–34; James Lloyd Breck: Apostle of the Wilderness, ed. Thomas C. Reeves (Nashotah, 1992), 50–51, 54–55

✠

Richard

Bishop of Chichester, 1253

A reading of excerpts from the Testament *and the* Prayer *of Richard, Bishop of Chichester, who died in 1253*

In the name of the Father, Son and Holy Ghost. Amen. I, Richard, by divine permission bishop of Chichester, constitute and make my testament in the underwritten manner.

In the first place, to the most high Trinity and to the blessed Mary I commend and bequeath my soul, and my body to be buried in the great church of Chichester in the nave of the same church, near the altar of the blessed Edmund of Abingdon, against the column.

Also to the fabric of the same church 40 pounds. Also to those who serve in the choir 5 pounds. Also my relics to the church of Chichester. Also to the Friars Minor of Chichester my psalter with commentary and 20 shillings. Also to the Friars Minor of Lewes a book of Gospels, namely Luke and John, and 20 shillings. Also to the Friars Minor of Winchelsea, Mark and Matthew and 20 shillings. Also to the Preaching Friars of Arundel, the book of Sentences [of Peter Lombard] and 20 shillings. Also to the Preaching Friars of Canterbury, Hosea with commentary and 20 shillings. Also to the Friars Minor of the same city Isaiah with commentary and 20 shillings. Also to the Preachers of London the book of Job, the Acts, the Canonical Epistles, the Apocalypse, all with commentary in one volume and 20 shillings. Also to the Friars Minor of the same city the Epistles of Paul with commentary and 20 shillings. Also to the Preaching Friars of Winchester the Summa of William of Auxerre and 20 shillings. Also to the Friars Minor of the same city the Twelve Prophets with commentary and 20 shillings. Also I bequeath in aid of the Holy Land 50 marks, to be paid and delivered to Robert Chaundos, my brother, in order that he may go there, if he is willing, for me, and to be paid to another, if the said Robert should be unwilling to go. Also to the abbey of Lacock my great cup of maplewood. Also to Friar Garin the books of John of Damascus with some others. Also to Friar William of Colchester, Preacher, the book of Anselm "Cur Deus Homo." Also to Friar Humphrey, the recluse of Pagham, 40 shillings. Also to the female recluse of Houghton half a mark. Also to the female recluse of Stopham half a mark. Also to the recluse of Hardham half a mark. Also to the female recluse of the Blessed Mary of Westoute at Lewes 5 shillings. Also to the brethren of the House of God at Dover 20 shillings for a pittance. Also to the monks of St. Martin of the same town one mark. Also to sir Simon de Terryng I bequeath my best palfrey and the book On Virtues, that is to say Distinctions on the Psalter. Also to sir William de Selsey, chaplain, my Bible. Also to Robert de Hastyng my Decretals. Also to sir William de Bramber, chaplain, a silver goblet and the book on Vices. Also to Henry, clerk of the chapel, 10 marks.

I will also that to carry out the foregoing bequests there be demanded from the lord king by my executors the profits of the bishopric of Chichester which he for two years took unjustly and which of right belong to me, for of them I will also seek payment even in the court of the Most High unless he has fully satisfied my executors.

I will also that if after my disposition set out above there is anything of my goods left over, let it be applied by my executors to help poor religious of my diocese, and to help hospitals, to repair bridges and roads, and to help widows, orphans and wards, as seems to them expedient.

I earnestly require my venerable father and lord, the archbishop of Canterbury, as principal executor and conservator of my goods (and, having asked permission, I constitute him principal executor and conservator of my goods) to direct, defend and deign to uphold against the opposition of disputants my underwritten will.

In witness of which matter, I have directed my seal to be affixed to the present writing.

Thanks be to you, my Lord Jesus Christ, for all the benefits you have won for me, for all the pains and insults you have borne for me. O most merciful redeemer, friend, and brother, may I know you more clearly, love you more dearly, and follow you more nearly, for ever and ever.

English Historical Documents 3, ed. Harry Rothwell (London, 1975), 776–779

APRIL 4 (OR JANUARY 15)

✠

Martin Luther King, Jr.

Civil Rights Leader, 1968

A reading from the sermon Loving your Enemies *preached by Martin Luther King, Jr., Civil Rights Leader, on Christmas of 1957 in Montgomery, Alabama*

Let us be practical and ask the question, How do we love our enemies?

First, we must develop and maintain the capacity to forgive. He who is devoid of the power to forgive is devoid of the power to love. It is impossible even to begin the act of loving one's enemies without the prior acceptance of the necessity, over and over again, of forgiving those who inflict evil and injury upon us. It is also necessary to realize that the forgiving act must always be initiated by the person who has been wronged.

Forgiveness does not mean ignoring what has been done or putting a false label on an evil act. It means, rather, that the evil act no longer remains as a barrier to the relationship. Forgiveness is a catalyst creating the atmosphere necessary for a fresh start and a new beginning. It is the lifting of a burden or the canceling of a debt. The words "I will forgive you, but I'll never forget what you've done" never explain the real nature of forgiveness. Certainly one can never forget, if that means erasing it totally from his mind. But when we forgive, we forget in the sense that the evil deed is no longer a mental block impeding a new relationship. Likewise, we can never say, "I will forgive you, but I won't have anything further to do with you." Forgiveness means reconciliation, a coming together again. Without this, no man can love his enemies. The degree to which we are able to forgive determines the degree to which we are able to love our enemies.

Second, we must recognize that the evil deed of the enemy-neighbor, the thing that hurts, never quite expresses all that he is. An element of goodness may be found even in our worst enemy. Each of us is something of a schizophrenic personality, tragically divided against ourselves. A persistent civil war rages within all of our lives.

This simply means that there is some good in the worst of us and some evil in the best of us. When we discover this, we are less prone to hate our enemies. When we look beneath the surface, beneath the impulsive evil deed, we see within our enemy-neighbor a measure of goodness and know that the viciousness and evilness of his acts are not quite representative of all that he is. We see him in a new light. We recognize that his hate grows out of fear, pride, ignorance, prejudice, and misunderstanding, but in spite of this, we know God's image is ineffably etched in his being.

Third, we must not seek to defeat or humiliate the enemy but to win his friendship and understanding. At times we are able to humiliate our worst enemy. Inevitably, his weak moments come and we are able to thrust in his side the spear of defeat. But this

78

we must not do. Every word and deed must contribute to an understanding with the enemy and release those vast reservoirs of goodwill which have been blocked by impenetrable walls of hate.

The relevance of what I have said to the crisis in race relations should be readily apparent. There will be no permanent solution to the race problem until oppressed men develop the capacity to love their enemies. The darkness of racial injustice will be dispelled only by the light of forgiving love. For more than three centuries American Negroes have been battered by the iron rod of oppression, frustrated by day and bewildered by night by unbearable injustice, and burdened with the ugly weight of discrimination. Forced to live with these shameful conditions, we are tempted to become bitter and to retaliate with a corresponding hate. But if this happens, the new order we seek will be little more than a duplicate of the old order. We must in strength and humility meet hate with love.

A.J. Muste Memorial Institute Essay Series, booklet no. 1 (N.Y., n.d.), 4–6, 10

APRIL 8

✜

William Augustus Muhlenberg
Priest, 1877

A reading from An Exposition of the Memorial *(regarding church unity) by William Augustus Muhlenberg, Priest, published in 1854*

Let our forms, for those who have been trained in them and for those who are drawn towards them, remain intact. Let the Prayer

Book be inviolate. Let the Episcopal Church stand as she does, only to flourish more and more in a green old age. Let our Right Reverend Fathers fulfil all their trust as her supreme guardians and pastors. Let them remit no part of that trust—but have they, have they not another, a higher trust? Is Protestant Episcopalianism just one and the same with the everlasting Gospel? In its Faith and Sacraments, yea. But in its practices, its ways, its usages, in the subordinate parts which go to make up its whole, is it part and parcel with God's dispensation for the salvation of mankind? Its own book, as we have just seen, repudiates the thought. Then our Bishops *have* another, a higher trust.

The Memorial submits the "practicability of an ecclesiastical system, broader and more comprehensive than that of the P.E. Church, including that Church as it now is, identical with that Church in all its great principles, yet providing for as much freedom in opinion, discipline, and worship, as is consistent with the essential faith and order of the Gospel." That our church, in the present form, will ever supply that grand desideratum, no man in his senses believes. There is nothing in her past history, nothing in the history of the whole church, nothing in the feeling of the denominations around us, nothing in the character of our countrymen, to give any encouragement to such an expectation. The great law, Diversity in Unity, forbids it. If there is ever to be an American Catholic church, that law will inevitably prevail. Were our Episcopal Church to become universal—if so extravagant a notion may be even put in words,—there would be unity indeed, but where would be the diversity? There would be a universal ecclesiastical sameness. All the varied developments of Christianity would be trimmed down to one and the same pattern.

The most to be hoped for, or desired, is expressed in that old true canon of Catholicity: "In necessary matters unity, in non-necessary matters liberty, in all things charity." The "necessary matters" of the church, are the Faith, the Ministry, the Sacraments, the Worship. Let these be Scriptural, and in accordance with the

Christianity of the Apostolic age, and we have the sum total of the elements of Catholic unity. With these secure, let the "Liberty in non-necessary matters" have its sway unrestrained in doctrine, discipline, worship, and opinion. In these, men will never be brought to think or act alike—never until the physical, the intellectual, and the moral world shall cease to exhibit the divers phenomena which have marked them since the creation. Diversity in unity is the universal law. In harmony with that law we *may* hope for a demonstration of the oneness of the Christian Church on this soil of freedom, where no political barriers stand in its way, and where the seekers of truth meet on equal and common ground. Who shall first move in such a demonstration? Who, but they that can do it with the most effect? Who, but they, without whom, it cannot be done at all?

An Exposition of the Memorial (N.Y., 1854), 39–40, 42–43

APRIL 9

✠

William Law
Priest, 1761

A reading from A Serious Call to a Devout and Holy Life *by William Law, Priest, published in 1728*

We readily acknowledge that God alone is to be the rule and measure of our prayers, that in them we are to look wholly unto Him and act wholly for Him, that we are only to pray in such a manner for such things and such ends as are suitable to His glory.

Now let anyone but find out the reason why he is to be thus strictly pious in his prayers and he will find the same as strong a reason to be as strictly pious in all the other parts of his life. For there is not the least shadow of a reason why we should make God the rule and measure of our prayers, why we should then look wholly unto Him and pray according to His will, but what equally proves it necessary for us to look wholly unto God, and make Him the rule and measure of all the other actions of our life. For any ways of life, any employment of our talents, whether of our parts, our time, or money, that is not strictly according to the will of God, that is not for such ends as are suitable to His glory, are as great absurdities and failings as prayers that are not according to the will of God. For there is no other reason why our prayers should be according to the will of God, why they should have nothing in them but what is wise, and holy, and heavenly, there is no other reason for this but that our lives may be of the same nature, full of the same wisdom, holiness, and heavenly tempers that we may live unto God in the same spirit that we pray unto Him. Were it not our strict duty to live by reason, to devote all the actions of our lives to God, were it not absolutely necessary to walk before Him in wisdom and holiness and all heavenly conversation, doing everything in His name and for His glory, there would be no excellency or wisdom in the most heavenly prayers. Nay, such prayers would be absurdities, they would be like prayers for wings when it was no part of our duty to fly.

There cannot anything be imagined more absurd in itself than wise and sublime and heavenly prayers added to a life of vanity and folly, where neither labor nor diversions, neither time nor money, are under the direction of the wisdom and heavenly tempers of our prayers. If we were to see a man pretending to act wholly with regard to God in everything that he did, that would neither spend time or money or take any labor or diversion but so far as he could act according to strict principles of reason and piety, and yet at the same time neglect all prayer, whether public or private, should we not be amazed at such a man and wonder how he could have so much folly along with so much religion?

Yet this is as reasonable as for any person to pretend to strictness in devotion, to be careful of observing times and places of prayer, and yet letting the rest of his life, his time and labor, his talents and money, be disposed of without any regard to strict rules of piety and devotion. For it is as great an absurdity to suppose holy prayers and divine petitions without a holiness of life suitable to them as to suppose a holy and divine life without prayers.

Edit. Paulist, 47–50

APRIL 11

✠

George Augustus Selwyn
Bishop of New Zealand, and of Lichfield, 1878

A reading from a sermon preached in Exeter Cathedral on Sunday, December 12, 1841, by George Augustus Selwyn before departing from England to become the first Bishop of New Zealand

The essential holiness of every part of the service of God; the immense privilege of being allowed either to minister in the name of Christ, or to enjoy the fruits of that ministry; the blessings of an established order of religious observances; and the comfort conveyed to the mind by visible tokens of the prevalence of a pure and spiritual faith: these are subjects for daily thankfulness, which too often escape men's observation, because of their customary recurrence. Those who have lived from their childhood in a Christian country, and have heard the Gospel preached every Lord's day, and have joined in the Church prayers until they know them almost by heart; and have been accustomed to look upon their clergyman as one of themselves, and to follow in the train of his teaching, as a matter of course, are apt to forget what a vast work of grace was necessary to procure for man the enjoyment of these ordinary benefits of a christian life.

Still more, when the house of God is opened daily for morning and evening prayer; when the Lord's song is sung without ceasing in strains of the purest and holiest melody: then it is that men are tempted most, by a spirit of self-dependence, to doubt the value of these ordinances of grace; to forget the power of continual intercession, and to think lightly of the duty of offering up to God an unceasing tribute of prayer and praise.

How shall *we* sing the Lord's song in a strange land, is a thought that comes home to our hearts now that we are about to depart, perhaps to return no more, nor see again our native country. We remember now, how from our earliest years our Church has nursed us in her bosom, as a hen gathereth her chickens under her wings; how the first prayers which we used were the words of our holy Mother; how the same guardian spirit watched over our growth in grace, confirming the promise of our baptism, and then inviting us to spiritual communion with Christ, and then the thought recurs, how often we have received that blessed sacrament of the body and blood of Christ with thankless hearts! how little we have thought of our vital union with Him in the body of His church; how feebly we have felt that we are in Him and He in us, that we are one with Him and He with us.

We remember how often in former days we have entered such venerable temples as this in which we are now assembled without awe at the thought that this is the house of God and the gate of heaven. We looked upon its clustered columns, and its high overhanging roof, and the symbol of the Cross traced out in the majestic symmetry of its outline, and its every line converging upward, as if the whole building were hung from heaven rather than based upon the earth: we once looked on these as the mere triumphs of human skill, but now they stand forth as the visible emblems of the majesty of the Church of Christ; as memorials of the self-denying zeal of the men of old; as the temples of the living God; as the glorious tombs of the saints of Christ; as the meeting-place of the spirits of the living with the spirits of the dead.

Again, we remember how often we have heard the Lord's song rising to heaven from within such choirs as this, where the priests and minstrels, as in the temple of old, sing to the Lord with a voice of melody, and make a cheerful noise unto the God of Jacob. But we never felt until now the value of the Lord's song, when the question comes home to our hearts, "How shall we sing the Lord's song in a strange land?"

Again, we remember the daily intercession offered up in these houses of prayer for the whole church of Christ. We once wondered at the perseverance of your prayers: when, sometimes, the priests and choristers were the only worshipers, we were tempted to question the value of your daily services; for we had not considered that the cathedral priest is a minister of the Eternal God, dependent not upon the caprice of man, but upon the commandment of Christ, who is the same yesterday, to-day, and for ever; that his duty is, to keep the watch of the Lord his God, even when others have forsaken Him.

"How shall we sing the Lord's song in a strange land?" Pray for us, that in the strange land to which we are called, we also may find in time the same spiritual comfort, and the same visible and outward aids to spiritual devotion. May we have both the spirit to preach the Gospel, and the strength to arise and build the temple of the Lord!

G. A. Selwyn. A Sermon preached in the Cathedral Church of St. Peter, Exeter, on Sunday, Dec. 12, 1841, previous to his departure from England (Exeter, 1842), 5–16

✠

Alphege

Archbishop of Canterbury, and Martyr, 1012

A reading from the Anglo-Saxon Chronicle *for the years 1011 and 1012, concerning the martyrdom of Alphege, Archbishop of Canterbury*

[The Danish invaders besieged Canterbury] and captured the Archbishop Alphege and all the ecclesiastics, and men and women—it was impossible for anyone to tell how many of the people that was—and they stayed afterwards in that borough as long as they pleased. And when they had then ransacked the whole borough, they went to their ships and took the archbishop with them.

He was then a captive who had been head of the English people and of Christendom. Misery could there be seen where happiness was often seen before, in that wretched city from which first came [to us] Christianity and happiness in divine and secular things. And they kept the archbishop with them till the time when they martyred him.

In this year Ealdorman Eadric and all the chief councillors of England, ecclesiastical and lay, came to London before Easter (Easter Sunday was on 13 April), and they stayed there until the tribute, namely 48,000 pounds, was all paid after Easter. Then on the Saturday the army became greatly incensed against the bishop because he would not promise them any money, but forbade that anything should be paid for him. They were also very drunk, for wine from the south had been brought there. They seized the bishop, and brought him to their assembly on the eve of the Sunday of the octave of Easter, which was 19 April, and shamefully put him to death there. They pelted him with bones and with ox-heads, and one of them struck him on the head with the back of an axe, so that he sank down with the blow, and his holy blood fell on the earth, while his sacred soul was sent to the realm of God. And in the morning his body was carried to London, and the bishops Eadnoth and Aelfhun and the citizens received it with all reverence and buried it in St. Paul's minster. And God now reveals there the powers of the holy martyr.

English Historical Documents 1, ed. Dorothy Whitelock (London, 1968), 222

APRIL 21

✠

Anselm

Archbishop of Canterbury, 1109

A reading of excerpts from the ontological argument for the existence of God, contained in the Proslogion *of Anselm, Archbishop of Canterbury, completed in 1079*

I began to ask myself if it would be possible to find one single argument, needing no other proof than itself, to prove that God really exists, that he is the highest good, needing nothing, that it is he whom all things need for their being and well-being, and to prove whatever else we believe about the nature of God. Lord, I do not seek to understand so that I may believe, but I believe so that I may understand.

Now, Lord, since it is you who gives understanding to faith, grant me to understand as well as you think fit, that you exist as we

87

believe, and that you are what we believe you to be. We believe that you are that thing than which nothing greater can be thought. Or is there nothing of that kind in existence, since "the fool has said in the heart, there is no God"? But when the fool hears me use this phrase, "something than which nothing greater can be thought," the fool understands what is heard; and what the fool understands is in the understanding, even if the fool does not understand that it exists. For it is one thing to have something in the understanding, but quite another to understand that it actually exists. It is like a painter who thinks out beforehand what is going to be created and has it in the understanding, but does not yet understand it as actually existing because it has not yet been painted. But when it has been painted, the painter both has it in the understanding and actually has it, because the painter has created it.

So the fool has to agree that the concept of something than which nothing greater can be thought exists in the understanding, since the fool understood what was heard and whatever is understood is in the understanding. And certainly that than which nothing greater can be thought cannot exist only in the understanding. For if it exists only in the understanding, it is possible to think of it existing also in reality, and that is greater. If that than which nothing greater can be thought exists in the understanding alone, then this thing than which nothing greater can be thought is something than which a greater can be thought. And this is clearly impossible. Therefore there can be no doubt at all that something than which a greater cannot be thought exists both in the understanding and in reality.

This being is yourself, our Lord and God.

Proslogion, preface, 1–3: Opera Omnia, ed. Schmitt, vol. 1

APRIL 29

✠

Catherine of Siena
1380

A reading from the works of Catherine of Siena, Dominican Sister and Mystic in the later fourteenth century

Make two dwelling-places for yourself, my daughter. One will be your actual cell, to keep you from wandering about from place to place except out of necessity, to obey your prioress, or for the sake of charity. Make the second dwelling-place a spiritual one that you take everywhere with you, namely the cell of true self-knowledge, wherein you will find knowledge of God's goodness [at work] in you. This second cell is really two cells in one, and when you are in one, you need to be in the other too, as otherwise your soul would fall into either confusion or presumption. Self-knowledge alone would result in confusion of mind, whereas to abide solely in knowledge of God would lead you to presumption. Each needs to be seasoned with the other and made into one and the same thing. If you do this, you will come to perfection.

A soul that yearns with great desire for God's honor and the salvation of souls, having trained itself for some time in the practice of virtue, and grown accustomed to dwell in the cell of self-knowledge, so as better to know the goodness of God in itself, is then led by love—since love is the consequence of knowledge—to seek the truth and to be clothed in it.

The sweet taste and light of this truth can in no way be approached so directly as through humble and unceasing prayer (based on knowledge of self and of God), for such prayer makes a soul one with God through following in the footsteps of Christ crucified, so that by ardent yearning and loving union the soul makes God to be its other self. Such seems to be Christ's teaching when he says: "To him who loves me and keeps my words I will manifest myself, and he shall become one with me and I with him." And in several places we find similar words which reveal to us the truth that through loving him the soul becomes another Christ.

Letter 33; The Dialogue of Divine Providence, prologue: ed. Foster and Ronayne (London, 1980), 151, 280

MAY 2

✠

Athanasius

Bishop of Alexandria, 373

A reading from the treatise On the Incarnation *written in the earlier fourth century by Athanasius, Bishop of Alexandria*

The Savior of us all, the Word of God, in his great love took to himself a body and moved as a human being among humans, drawing toward himself all human senses, so that those who were seeking God in corporeal things might apprehend the Father through the works which he, the Word of God, did in the body. Human and human-minded as they were, to whichever side they looked in the sensible world, they found themselves being taught the truth. Were they awe-stricken by creation? They beheld it confessing Christ as Lord. Did their minds tend to regard humans as gods? The uniqueness of the Savior's works marked him, alone of human beings, as Son of God. Were they drawn to evil spirits? They saw them driven out by the Lord and learned that the Word of God alone was God and that the evil spirits were not gods at all. Were they inclined to hero-worship and the cult of the dead? Then the fact that the Savior had risen from the dead showed them how false these other deities were, and that the Word of the Father is the one true Lord, the Lord even of death. For this reason was he both born and manifested as human, for this he died and rose, in order that, eclipsing by his works all other human deeds, he might recall humanity from all the paths of error to know the Father. As he says himself: "I came to seek and to save that which was lost."

When, then, human minds had fallen finally to the level of corporeal things, the Word submitted to appear in a body, in order that he, as human, might focus their senses on himself and convince them through his human acts that he himself is not only human but also God, the Word and Wisdom of the true God. This is what Paul wants to tell us when he says: "That you, being rooted and grounded in love, may be strong to apprehend with all the saints what is the length and breadth and height and depth, and to know the love of God that surpasses knowledge, so that you may be filled with all the fulness of God." The self-revealing of the Word is in every dimension: above, in creation; below, in the incarnation; in the depth, in hades; in the breadth, throughout the world. All things have been filled with the knowledge of God.

For this reason he did not offer the sacrifice on behalf of all immediately after he came, for if he had surrendered his body to death and then raised it again at once he would have ceased to be an object of our senses. Instead of that, he stayed in his body and let himself be seen in it, doing acts and giving signs which showed him to be not only human but also God the Word. There were thus two things which the Savior did for us by becoming as we are. He banished death from us and made us anew; and, invisible and imperceptible as in himself he is, he became visible through his works and revealed himself as the Word of the Father, the ruler and king of all.

Even the very creation broke silence at his behest and, marvelous to relate, confessed with one voice before the cross, that monument of victory, that he who suffered thereon in the body was not human only but Son of God and Savior of all. The sun veiled its face, the earth quaked, the mountains were rent asunder, everyone was struck with awe. These things showed that Christ on the cross was God, and that all creation was his servant and was bearing witness by its deference to the presence of its master.

On the Incarnation 15–16, 19: PG 25, 121–124, 129–130

MAY 4

✠

Monnica

Mother of Augustine of Hippo, 387

A reading from the Confessions *of Augustine, Bishop of Hippo, concerning his mother, Monnica, who died in the year 387*

The day was now approaching when my mother Monnica would depart from this life; you knew that day, Lord, though we did not. She and I happened to be standing by ourselves at a window that overlooked the garden in the courtyard of the house. At the time we were in Ostia on the Tiber.

As the flame of love burned stronger in us and raised us higher toward the eternal God, our thoughts ranged over the whole compass of material things in their various degrees, up to the heavens themselves, from which the sun and the moon and the stars shine down upon the earth. Higher still we climbed, thinking and speaking all the while in wonder at all that you have made. At length we came to our own souls and passed beyond them to that place of everlasting plenty, where you feed Israel for ever with the food of truth. There life is that Wisdom by which all these things that we know are made, all things that ever have been and all that are yet to be. But that Wisdom is not made; it is as it has always been and as it will be for ever—or, rather, I should not say that it "has been" or "will be," for it simply "is," because eternity is not in the past or in the future. And while we spoke of the eternal wisdom, longing for it and straining for it with all the strength of our hearts, for one fleeting instant we reached out and touched it. Then with a sigh, we returned to the sound of our own speech, in which each word has a beginning and an ending—far, far different from your word, our Lord, who abides in himself for ever, yet never grows old and gives new life to all things.

Then my mother said: "My son, for my part I find no further pleasure in this life. What I am still to do or why I am here in the world, I do not know, for I have no further hopes on this earth. There was one reason, and one alone, why I wished to remain a little longer in this life, and that was to see you become a catholic Christian before I died. God has granted my wish and more besides, for I now see you as his servant, spurning such happiness as the world can give. What is left for me to do in this world?"

I scarcely remember what answer I gave her. It was about five days after this, or not much more, that she took to her bed with a fever. One day during her illness she had a fainting spell and lost consciousness for a short time. We hurried to her bedside, but she soon regained consciousness and looked up at my brother and me as we stood beside her. With a puzzled look she asked: "Where was I?"

Then she went on: "It does not matter where you bury my body. Do not let that worry you! All I ask of you is that, wherever you may be, you should remember me at the altar of the Lord."

Although she hardly had the strength to speak, she managed to make us understand her wishes and then fell silent, for her illness was becoming worse and she was in great pain. And so, on the ninth day of her illness, when she was fifty-six and I was thirty-three, her pious and devoted soul was set free from the body.

What was it, then, that caused me such deep sorrow? It can only have been because the wound was fresh, the wound I had received when our life together, which had been so precious and so dear to me, was suddenly cut off. I found comfort in the memory that as I did what I could for my mother in the last stages of her illness, she had caressed me and said that I was a good son to her.

When the body was carried out for burial, I went and returned without a tear. I did not weep even during the prayers which we recited while the Sacrifice of our redemption was offered for my mother and her body rested by the grave before it was laid in the earth, as is the custom there. Yet all that day I was secretly weighed down with grief.

She had no care whether her body was to be buried in a rich shroud or embalmed with spices, nor did she wish to have a special monument or a grave in her own country. These were not the last wishes she passed on to us. All she wanted was that we should remember her at your altar, where she had been your servant day after day, without fail.

O my Lord my God, inspire your servants who read this book to remember Monnica, your servant, at your altar and with her Patricius, her husband, who died before her, by whose bodies you brought me into this life, though how it was I do not know. With pious hearts let them remember those who were not only my parents in this light that fails, but were also my brother and sister, subject to you, our Father, in our catholic mother the church, and will be my fellow citizens in the eternal Jerusalem for which your people sigh throughout their pilgrimage, from the time when they set out until the time when they return to you.

Confessions 9, 10–12: CSEL 33, 215–219

MAY 8

✠

Dame Julian of Norwich
c. 1417

A reading from the Revelations of Divine Love *by Dame Julian of Norwich, being an account of revelation number 13, received on 8 May 1373*

Jesus, who in this vision informed me of all I needed, answered: "Sin was necessary—but it is all going to be all right; it is all going to be all right; everything is going to be all right." In this simple word "sin" our Lord reminded me in a general sort of way of all that is not good: the despicable shame and utter self-denial he endured for us, both in his life and in his dying, and of all the suffering and pain of his creation, both spiritual and physical. For all of us have already experienced something of this abnegation and we have to deny ourselves as we follow our master, Jesus, until we are wholly cleansed. I mean, until this body of death and our inward affections (which are not very good) are completely done away. All this I saw, together with all the suffering that ever has been or can be. And of all pain I understood that the passion of Christ was the greatest and most surpassing. All this was shown in a flash, and quickly passed over into consolation—for our good Lord would not have the soul frightened by this ugly sight.

But I did not see "sin." I believe it has no substance or real existence. It can only be known by the pain it causes. This pain is something, as I see it, which lasts but a while. It purges us and makes us know ourselves, so that we ask for mercy. The passion of our Lord is our comfort against all this—for such is his blessed will. Because of his tender love for all those who are to be saved our good Lord comforts us at once and sweetly, as if to say: "It is true

95

that sin is the cause of all this pain; but it is all going to be all right; it is all going to be all right; everything is going to be all right." These words were said most tenderly, with never a hint of blame either to me or to any of those to be saved. It would be most improper of me therefore to blame or criticize God for my sin, since he does not blame me for it.

In these words I saw one of God's marvelously deep secrets—a secret which he will plainly reveal to us in heaven. And when we know it, we will see the reason why he allowed sin to come, and seeing, we shall rejoice in him for ever.

This being so, I thought it quite impossible that everything should turn out well, as our Lord was now showing me. But I had no answer to this revelation save this: "What is impossible to you is not impossible to me. I shall honor my word in every respect, and I will make everything turn out for the best." Thus was I taught by God's grace to hold steadfastly to the faith I had already learned, and at the same time to believe quite seriously that everything would turn out all right, as our Lord was showing. For the great deed that our Lord is going to do is that by which he shall keep his word in every particular, and make all that is wrong turn out well. How this will be no one less than Christ can know—not until the deed is done.

Revelation 13, chapters 27, 32: Colledge and Walsh 2, 405–407, 425–426

Gregory of Nazianzus

Bishop of Constantinople, 389

A reading from the Second Theological Oration, *on* God, *preached in the summer or fall of 380 by Gregory of Nazianzus, Bishop of Constantinople*

What God is in nature and essence, no-one ever yet has discovered or can discover. Whether it will ever be discovered is a question which whoever wishes may examine and decide. In my opinion it will be discovered when that within us which is godlike and divine, I mean our mind and reason, shall have mingled with its like, and the image shall have ascended to the archetype, of which it has now the desire.

If you have in your thought passed through the air and all the things of air, reach with me to heaven and the things of heaven. And let faith lead us rather than reason, if at least you have learned the feebleness of the latter in matters nearer to you, and have known reason by knowing the things that are beyond reason, so as not to be altogether on the earth or of the earth, because you are ignorant even of your ignorance.

Who spread the sky around us, and set the stars in order? Or rather, first, can you tell me, of your own knowledge of the things in heaven, what are the sky and the stars; you who know not what lies at your very feet, and cannot even take the measure of yourself, and yet must busy yourself about what is above your nature, and gape at that which is limitless?

How came the sun to be a beacon fire to the whole world, and to all eyes like the leader of some chorus, concealing all the rest of the stars by its brightness, more completely than some of them conceal others? The proof of this is that they shine against the sun, but it out-shines them and does not even allow it to be perceived that they rose simultaneously with it, fair as a bridegroom, swift and great as a giant. The sun is so mighty in strength that from one end to the other of the world it embraces all things in its heat, and there is nothing hid from the feeling thereof, but it fills both every eye with light, and every embodied creature with heat, warming, yet not burning, by the gentleness of its temper and the order of its movement, present to all, and equally embracing all.

Have you considered the importance of the fact that [Plato] speaks of the sun as holding the same position among material objects as God does among objects of thought? For the one gives light to the eyes, as the other does to the mind; and is the most beautiful of the objects of sight, as God is of those of thought. But who gave to the sun motion at first? And what is it which ever moves the sun in its circuit, though in its nature stable and immovable, truly unwearied, and the giver and sustainer of life, and all the rest of the titles which the poets justly sing of the sun, and never resting in its course or its benefits? How comes the sun to be the creator of day when above the earth, and of night when below it?

How comes the sun to be the maker and divider of the seasons, that come and depart in regular order, and as in a dance interweave with each other, or stand apart by a law of love on the one hand and of order on the other, and mingle little by little, and steal on their neighbor, just as nights and days do, so as not to give us pain by their suddenness? This will be enough about the sun.

Do you know the nature and phenomena of the moon, and the measures and courses of light, and how it is that the sun bears rule over the day, and the moon presides over the night; and while the moon gives confidence to wild beasts, the sun stirs man up to work, raising or lowering as may be most serviceable? Know you the bond of Pleiades, or the fence of Orion, as the one who counts the number of the stars and calls them all by their names? Know you the differences of the glory of each, and the order of their movement, that I should trust you, when by them you weave the web of human concerns, and arm the creature against the Creator?

If we have told these things as they deserve, it is by the grace of the Trinity, and of the one Godhead in three Persons; but if less perfectly than we have desired, yet even so our discourse has gained its purpose. For this is what we were laboring to show, that even the secondary natures surpass the power of our intellect.

Second Theological Oration, 17, 28–31: PG 36, 47–48, 65–75

MAY 19

✠

Dunstan

Archbishop of Canterbury, 988

A reading from the earliest form of the Coronation Oath from the first English Coronation Service, composed by Dunstan, Archbishop of Canterbury, in the year 973

Three things I promise in Christ's name to the Christian people subject to me: First, that the church of God and the whole Christian people shall have true peace at all time by our judgment. Second, that I will forbid extortion and all kinds of wrong-doing to all orders of persons. Third, that I will enjoin equity and mercy in all judgments, so that God, who is kind and merciful, may vouchsafe his mercy to me and to you.

"Zadok the priest and Nathan the prophet anointed Solomon king, and all the people rejoiced and said: Long live the king for ever. The king shall rejoice in your strength, O Lord, and in your help the king shall greatly exult." [I Kings 1.45; Psalm 21.1]

E. C. Ratcliff. The Coronation Service of Her Majesty Queen Elizabeth II (London, 1953), 9, 24

MAY 20

✠

Alcuin

Deacon, and Abbot of Tours, 804

A reading from the epitaph composed by Alcuin, Deacon and Abbot of Tours, for his own tomb, before his death in the year 804

Pause here, I pray you, for a little while, O wayfarer, and ponder what I have written, so that you may learn by my fate what yours shall be. What you are now, O wayfarer of world renown, I was, and what I am now so you shall be. The world's delights I followed in empty love, but now I am ashes and dust, food for worms.

Wherefore give attention to your soul rather than to your flesh, for the former remains, the latter dies. Why do you cultivate the open fields? You can see that repose here holds me in this small chamber, and it will be the same for you. Why do you long for your body to be vested in purple crimson? The worm is hungry for that body's meat! Just as the flowers die when a harsh wind comes, even so with your flesh, all its glory shall pass away.

Now, reader, I ask you, take your turn in song, and say, I pray: "Give pardon to this your servant, O Christ." May no hand violate the sacred bounds of this sepulchre until the angelic trumpet sounds from the height: "Arise from the grave, you who lie in the tomb, the great judge of unnumbered hosts is here at hand."

Alcuin was my name and learning was my love. Extend your prayers on my behalf, you who read these lines.

Gerard Ellard. Master Alcuin, Liturgist (Chicago, 1956), 215–216

M A Y   2 4

✠

Jackson Kemper

First Missionary Bishop in the United States, 1870

A reading from the Triennial Sermon *of Jackson Kemper, First Missionary Bishop in the United States, preached before the Board of Missions in 1841*

How remarkably peculiar, how vastly important is the position of our Church! Possessing as we fully believe all those characteristics which distinguished the primitive fold:—A scriptural Liturgy—evangelical doctrines—and the apostolic succession—having the form of godliness *and* the power thereof—free from the false and worldly scruples and the time-serving policy of civil governments—independent—respected, and influential—in the midst of an intelligent, enterprising and commercial people—Brethren! may it not be *our* duty to convert the world—may not this high, this inestimable privilege be offered to *us!* And are we prepared—are we doing at the present moment *even one tenth* part of what we are capable? Our means and our power are extensive—and under the blessing of Him, without whom nothing is strong, nothing is holy, our aim—our constant, undeviating, untiring aim should be great and lofty. "Glorious things are spoken of thee, O city of God."

With the talents we possess, (and for which, as good stewards, we must finally account, at that hour when no secrets can be hid), with the talents committed to our trust and the privileges we enjoy, cannot our faith, our liberality and our self-denial, *greatly* increase? Cannot our supplications be more fervent, our economy more strict, our love of souls more ardent? Have we, as individuals, or a Church, a deep and abiding interest in the success of missions?

Not a brother would I accuse of indifference or cowardice. But I would stir up, with God's permission, the pure mind of each one, by way of remembrance. It is the spirit of missions I earnestly and most affectionately advocate.

The division into Foreign and Domestic is often arbitrary, and might, without detriment, be abolished; for no one, I presume, would wish to withdraw our heralds of the cross from Africa, suspend our incipient efforts for Texas, or abandon the much injured aborigines to all the degrading vices they have learnt from unprincipled men who pretend to be civilized. Let us go where duty calls—where Providence points the way—and let us rejoice in the privilege, for we assuredly ought—O, let us rejoice in the privilege of sending forth in the name of the Lord and under the guidance of *his* Spirit *all* those, who, thoroughly instructed in sacred truths, hear the cry, Come over and help us—and *cannot* resist the deep, the abiding conviction concerning their sphere of duty—whose hearts burn within them when they hear of people or nations wholly given to idolatry, or licentiousness, or worldly-mindedness. Cultivate, dear brethren of the clergy, cultivate with the utmost assiduity your own vineyard—love with the strongest affection your own spiritual children,—but close not your hearts to the sufferings and the wants of your neighbors.

Triennial Sermon before the Board of Missions (N.Y., 1841), 8–9

✠

Bede, the Venerable

Priest, and Monk of Jarrow, 735

A reading of excerpts from the beginning and the ending of the Ecclesiastical History of England *by Bede the Venerable, Priest and Monk of Jarrow, who died in the year 735*

Some while ago, at your Majesty's request, I gladly sent you the history of the English church and people which I had recently completed. I warmly welcome your eager desire to know something of the doings and sayings of those who have lived in the past, and of the famous of our own nation in particular. For if history records good things of good people, the thoughtful hearer is encouraged to imitate what is good; or if it records evil things of the wicked, the devout and religious listener or reader is encouraged to avoid all that is sinful and perverse and to follow what is good and pleasing to God.

With God's help, I, Bede, the servant of Christ and priest of the monastery of the blessed apostles Peter and Paul at Wearmouth and Jarrow, have assembled these facts about the history of the church in Britain, and of the church of the English in particular, so far as I have been able to ascertain them from ancient writings, from the traditions of our forebears, and from my own personal knowledge.

I was born on the lands of this monastery, and on reaching seven years of age, I was entrusted by my family first to the most reverend Abbot Benedict and later to Abbot Ceolfrid for my education. I have spent all the remainder of my life in this monastery and devoted myself entirely to the study of the Scriptures. And while I have observed the regular discipline and sung the choir offices daily in church, my chief delight has always been in study, teaching, and writing.

I was ordained deacon in my nineteenth year, and priest in my thirtieth, receiving both these orders at the hands of the most reverend Bishop John at the direction of Abbot Ceolfrid. From the time of my receiving the priesthood until my fifty-ninth year, I have worked, both for my own benefit and that of my brethren, to compile short extracts from the works of the venerable Fathers on Holy Scripture and to comment on their meaning and interpretation.

I pray you, noble Jesu, that as you have graciously granted me joyfully to imbibe the words of your knowledge, so you will also of your bounty grant me to come at length to yourself, the fount of all wisdom, and to dwell in your presence for ever.

Ecclesiastical History, preface and 5, 24: Colgrave and Mynors, 2–3, 566–567, 570–571

MAY 26

✠

Augustine

First Archbishop of Canterbury, 605

A reading from the Ecclesiastical History *of Bede the Venerable, Priest and Monk of Jarrow, concerning the arrival of Augustine, first Archbishop of Canterbury, to England in the year 597*

Augustine and his fellow-servants of Christ resumed their work in the word of God, and arrived in Britain. At this time the most powerful king there was Ethelbert, who reigned in Kent and whose domains extended northwards to the river Humber. He had already heard of the Christian religion, having a Christian wife of the Frankish royal house named Bertha, whom he had received from her parents on condition that she should have freedom to hold and practice her faith unhindered with [the assistance of] Bishop Liudhard, whom they had sent as her helper in the faith.

After some days, the king came to the island [of Thanet] and, sitting down in the open air, summoned Augustine and his companions to an audience. But he took precautions that they should not approach him in a house; for he held an ancient superstition that, if they were practisers of magical arts, they might have opportunity to deceive and master him. But the monks were endowed with power from God, not from the devil, and they approached the king carrying a silver cross as their standard and the likeness of our Lord and Savior painted on a board. First of all they offered prayer to God, singing a litany for the eternal salvation both of themselves and of those to whom and for whose sake they had come. And when, at the king's command, they had sat down and preached the word of life to the king and his court, the king said: "Your words and promises are fair indeed; but they are new and uncertain, and I cannot accept them and abandon the age-old beliefs that I have held together with the whole English nation. But since you have traveled far, and I càn see that you are sincere in your desire to impart to us what you believe to be true and excellent, we will not harm you. We will receive you hospitably and take care to supply you with all that you need; nor will we forbid you to preach and win any people you can to your religion."

The king then granted them a dwelling in the city of Canterbury, which was the chief city of all his realm, and in accordance with his promise he allowed them provisions and did not withdraw their freedom to preach. Tradition says that as they approached the city, bearing the holy cross and the likeness of our great King and Lord Jesus Christ as was their custom, they sang in unison this litany: "We pray you, O Lord, in all your mercy, that your wrath and anger

105

may be turned away from this city and from your holy house, for we are sinners. Alleluia."

As soon as they had occupied the house given to them they began to emulate the life of the apostles and the primitive church. They were constantly at prayer; they fasted and kept vigils; they preached the word of life to whomsoever they could. They regarded worldly things as of little importance, and accepted only the necessities of life from those they taught. They practiced what they preached, and were willing to endure any hardship, and even to die for the truth which they proclaimed. Before long a number of heathen, admiring the simplicity of their holy lives and the comfort of their heavenly message, believed and were baptized.

On the east side of the city stood an old church, built in honor of Saint Martin during the Roman occupation of Britain, where the Christian queen of whom I have spoken went to pray. Here they first assembled to sing the psalms, to pray, to say Mass, to preach, and to baptize, until the king's own conversion to the Faith gave them greater freedom to preach and to build and restore churches everywhere.

Ecclesiastical History 1, 25–26: Colgrave and Mynors, 72–77

MAY–JUNE

✠

The First Book of Common Prayer
1549

A reading from the original Preface to the First Book of Common Prayer, written by Thomas Cranmer, Archbishop of Canterbury, in the year 1549

There was never any thing by the wit of man so well devised, or so sure established, which in continuance of time hath not been corrupted: as, among other things, it may plainly appear by the common prayers in the Church, commonly called Divine Service: the first original and ground whereof, if a man would search out by the ancient fathers, he shall find, that the same was not ordained, but of a good purpose, and for a great advancement of godliness: For they so ordered the matter, that all the whole Bible (or the greatest part thereof) should be read over once in the year, intending thereby, that the Clergy, and especially such as were Ministers of the congregation, should (by often reading, and meditation of God's word) be stirred up to godliness themselves, and be more able to exhort others by wholesome doctrine, and to confute them that were adversaries to the truth. And further, that the people (by daily hearing of holy Scripture read in the Church) should continually profit more and more in the knowledge of God, and be the more inflamed with the love of his true religion.

Book of Common Prayer (U.S.A., 1979), p. 866 ff.

JUNE 1

✠

Justin
Martyr at Rome, c. 167

A reading from the First Apology *of Justin, Martyr at Rome, written c. 155*

When you hear that we look for a kingdom, you rashly suppose that we mean something merely human. But we speak of a kingdom with God, as is clear from our confessing Christ when you bring us to trial, though we know that death is the penalty for this confession. For if we looked for a human kingdom we would deny it in order to save our lives, and would try to remain in hiding in order to obtain the things we look for. But since we do not place our hopes on the present, we are not troubled by being put to death, since we will have to die somehow in any case.

We are in fact of all people your best helpers and allies in securing good order, convinced as we are that no wicked person, no covetous person or conspirator, or virtuous one either, can be hidden from God, and that everyone goes to eternal punishment or salvation in accordance with the character of their actions. If everyone knew this, nobody would choose vice even for a little time.

We, however, after thus washing those who have been convinced and signified assent, lead them to those who are called "brethren," where they are assembled. They then earnestly offer common prayers for themselves and the one who has been illuminated and all others everywhere that we may be made worthy, having learned the truth, to be found in deed good citizens and keepers of what is commanded, so that we may be saved with eternal salvation. On finishing the prayers we greet each other with a kiss. Then bread and a cup of water and mixed wine are brought to the one who presides and the presider, taking them, sends up praise and glory to the Father of the universe through the name of the Son and of the Holy Spirit, and offers thanksgiving at some length that we have been deemed worthy to receive these things. When the presider has finished the prayers and the thanksgiving, the whole congregation assents, saying: "Amen." "Amen" in the Hebrew language means: "So be it." When the presider has given thanks and the whole congregation has assented, those whom we call deacons give to each of those present a portion of the consecrated bread and wine and water, and they take it to the absent.

First Apology 11–12, 65: PG 6, 341–342, 427–428

JUNE 2

✠

The Martyrs of Lyons
177

A reading from the Letter of the Churches of Lyons and Vienne *concerning the martyrdom of Blandina and her companions in the year 177*

The whole fury of crowd, governor, and soldiers fell with crushing force on Sanctus, the deacon from Vienne, on Maturus, very recently baptized but heroic in facing his ordeal; on Attakus, who had always been a pillar and support of the church in his native Pergamon; and on Blandina, through whom Christ proved that things which people regard as mean, unlovely, and contemptible are by God deemed worthy of great glory, because of her love for God shown in power and not vaunted in appearance.

When we were all afraid, and her earthly mistress, who was herself facing the ordeal of martyrdom, was in agony lest she should be unable even to make a bold confession of Christ because of bodily weakness, Blandina was filled with such power that those who took it in turns to subject her to every kind of torture from morning to night were exhausted by their efforts and confessed themselves beaten. They could think of nothing else to do to her. They were amazed that she was still breathing, for her whole body was mangled and her wounds gaped. They declared that torment of any one kind was enough to divide soul and body, let alone a succession of torments of such extreme severity. But the blessed woman, wrestling magnificently, grew in strength as she proclaimed her faith, and found refreshment, rest, and insensibility to her sufferings in uttering the words: "I am a Christian: we do nothing to be ashamed of."

June 2

Blandina was hung on a post and exposed as food for the wild beasts let loose in the arena. She looked as if she was hanging in the form of a cross, and through her ardent prayers she stimulated great enthusiasm in those undergoing their ordeal, who in their agony saw with their outward eyes in the person of their sister the One who was crucified for them, that He might convince those who believe in Him that any one who has suffered for the glory of Christ has fellowship for ever with the living God.

To crown all this, on the last day of the sports Blandina was again brought in, and with her Ponticus, a lad of about fifteen. Day after day they had been taken in to watch the rest being punished, and attempts were made to make them swear by the heathen idols. When they stood firm and treated these efforts with contempt, the mob was infuriated with them, so that the boy's tender age called forth no pity and the woman no respect. They subjected them to every horror and inflicted every punishment in turn, attempting again and again to make them swear, but to no purpose. Ponticus was encouraged by his sister in Christ, so that the heathen saw that she was urging him on and stiffening his resistance, and he bravely endured every punishment till he gave back his spirit to God.

Last of all, like a noble mother who had encouraged her children and sent them before her in triumph to the king, blessed Blandina herself passed through all the ordeals of her children and hastened to rejoin them, rejoicing and exulting at her departure as if invited to a wedding supper, not thrown to the beasts. After the whips, after the beasts, after the griddle, she was finally dropped into a basket and thrown to a bull. Time after time the animal tossed her, but she was indifferent now to all that happened to her, because of her hope and sure hold on all that her faith meant, and of her communing with Christ. Then she, too, was sacrificed, while the heathen themselves admitted that never yet had they known a woman suffer so much or so long.

Eusebius, Ecclesiastical History 5, 1: PG 20, 416, 425, 432

JUNE 3

✠

The Martyrs of Uganda
1886

A reading from the story of the Uganda martyrs and their last words in 1886

The cortège was then assembled and, shortly after, set out on what was to be for most of the prisoners their last journey on earth, the journey to Namugongo.

The choice of Namugongo as the scene for their martyrdom seems to have been due to the fact that most of the victims were royal liege-men or pages. This site had been set aside for the execution of princes during the reign of Kabaka Kyabagu, some hundred years before, and ever since then had been reserved mainly for the execution of persons of royal blood, chiefs, and others of importance.

As they went along, words of encouragement were passed backwards and forwards along the line. "Then we talked of God," says Kamyuka, "and said to one another: 'First to offer oneself to do a good act and then to omit it, is playing the fool and the coward. The day has come for us to make good our promise. Let us die bravely for the cause of God'."

Another subject discussed by the martyrs as they trudged along the dusty road was the constancy of the newly baptized. "Friends," said some of those who had been baptized by the priests to those baptized by Charles Lwanga, "we were afraid that you people would deny your religion." "Deny our religion!" exclaimed the young pages, "Have not we given ourselves to Jesus Christ as well as you?"

[*The following is recorded in the account of Denis Kamyuka:*]

111

June 3

At Namugongo there was a prison, but we were not confined in it. Mukajanga ordered the executioners to lodge us in their enclosures throughout the village. As we separated to be taken to our lodgings, those who had been the first to become Christians said to us, "You have heard that our friends have been put to death. They are now with Jesus Christ. Let us remain firm like them, and we too shall go where they have gone, to Jesus Christ." Those who inspired us with courage were Charles Lwanga, Bruno Serunkuma, James Buzabaliawo and Anatole Kiriggwajjo. Then the executioners took us away. I shared a hut with my friends Gyavira and Mugagga. They put our necks in rings which were then fastened to the posts of the hut.

Having removed the stocks, slave-yokes and rings from their prisoners' limbs and necks, the guards tied their hands behind their backs and led them out into the open space before the chief executioner's house.

When the executioners began to strap him down, Charles Lwanga said to them, "Will you please untie me and allow me to arrange the pyre myself?" His request was granted, and the martyr arranged his own death-bed of firewood. Then lying down, he was tied and strapped as before. Senkole lit a torch of grass from the Sacred Fuse and set fire to the wood under the martyr's feet. Slowly the flames burnt his feet and legs to charred bones, leaving the rest of his body unharmed. Senkole, as he went about his task of controlling the fire so that it should not spread too quickly, said to Charles, "Ah, let me punish you properly, and let us see whether your God will come and deliver you from the fire." Charles, bearing his agony without a murmur, replied, "You poor foolish man! You do not understand what you are saying. You are burning me, but it is as if you were pouring water over my body. I am dying for God's religion. But be warned in time, or God whom you insult will one day plunge you into real fire."

After this exchange, Charles lay quietly, praying and waiting for the moment when his soul should be set free from his tortured body. The fire spread slowly. Just before it finally stopped the beating of his heart, Charles Lwanga cried out in a loud voice, "Katonda! (My God)," and so died.

J. F. Faupel. African Holocaust: The Story of the Uganda Martyrs (London and New York, 1962), 168, 169, 171, 191, 193

JUNE 5

✠

Boniface

Archbishop of Mainz, Missionary to Germany, and Martyr, 754

A reading from a letter of Boniface, Archbishop of Mainz and Missionary to Germany, who died as a martyr in the year 754

In her voyage across the ocean of this world, the church is like a great ship being pounded by the waves of life's different stresses. Our duty is not to abandon ship but to keep her on her course.

The ancient fathers showed us how we should carry out this duty: Clement, Cornelius and many others in the city of Rome, Cyprian at Carthage, Athanasius at Alexandria. They all lived under emperors who were pagans; they all steered Christ's ship—or rather his most dear spouse, the church. This they did by teaching and defending her, by their labors and sufferings, even to the shedding of blood.

I am terrified when I think of all this. "Fear and trembling came upon me and the darkness" of my sins "almost covered me." I would gladly give up the task of guiding the church which I have accepted if I could find such an action warranted by the example of the fathers or by Holy Scripture.

Since this is the case, and since the truth can be assaulted but never defeated or falsified, with our tired mind let us turn to the words of Solomon: "Trust in the Lord with all your heart and do not rely on your own prudence. Think on him in all your ways, and he will guide your steps." In another place he says: "The name of the Lord is an impregnable tower. The just seek refuge in it and will be saved."

Let us stand fast in what is right and prepare our souls for trial. Let us wait upon God's strengthening aid and say: "O Lord, you have been our refuge from one generation to another."

Let us trust in the One who has placed this burden upon us. What we ourselves cannot bear let us bear with the help of Christ. For he is all-powerful and he tells us: "My yoke is easy and my burden is light."

Let us be neither dogs that do not bark nor silent onlookers nor paid servants who run away before the wolf. Instead let us be careful shepherds watching over Christ's flock. Let us preach the whole of God's plan to the powerful and to the humble, to rich and to poor, to persons of every rank and age, as far as God gives us the strength, in season and out of season, as Saint Gregory writes in his Book on Pastoral Care.

Letter 78: MGH Epistolae 3, 352, 354

JUNE 9

✠

Columba

Abbot of Iona, 597

A reading about Columba, Priest and first Abbot of Iona in the mid-sixth century, from the Ecclesiastical History *of Bede the Venerable, Priest and Monk of Jarrow*

Columba arrived in Britain in the ninth year of the reign of the powerful Pictish king, Bride son of Meilochon. He converted that people to the faith of Christ by his preaching and example, and received from them the island of Iona on which to found a monastery. Iona is a small island, with an area of about five hides according to English reckoning. It was here that Columba died and was buried at the age of seventy-seven, some thirty-two years after he had come into Britain to preach. Before he came to Britain, he had founded a noble monastery in Ireland known in the Scots language as "Dearmach," the Field of Oaks, because of the oak forest in which it stands. From both of these monasteries Columba's disciples went out and founded many others in Britain and Ireland; but the monastery on the isle of Iona, where his body lies, remains the chief of them all.

Iona is always ruled by an abbot in priest's orders, to whose authority the whole province, including the bishops, is subject, contrary to the usual custom. This practice was established by its first abbot Columba, who was not a bishop himself, but a priest and monk.

Columba was the first teacher of the Christian faith to the Picts living north of the mountains, and founder of the monastery on the Isle of Iona, which long remained venerated by the peo-

115

ple of the Picts and Scots. For this reason, Columba is now known by some people as Columbkill, a name compounded from "Columba" and "cell."

Ecclesiastical History 3, 4; 5, 9: Colgrave and Mynors, 222–225, 478–479

JUNE 10

✠

Ephrem of Edessa, Syria
Deacon, 373

A reading from a sermon of Ephrem of Edessa, Syria, Deacon and poet in the mid-fourth century

Lord, shed upon our darkened souls the brilliant light of your wisdom so that we may be enlightened and serve you with renewed purity. Sunrise marks the hour for our toil to begin, but in our souls, Lord, prepare a dwelling for the day that will never end. Grant that we may come to know the risen life and that nothing may distract us from the delights you offer. Through our unremitting zeal for you, Lord, set upon us the sign of your day that is not measured by the sun.

In your sacrament we daily embrace you and receive you into our bodies. Make us worthy to experience the resurrection for which we hope. We have had your treasure hidden within us ever since we received baptismal grace. It grows ever richer at your sacramental table. Teach us to find our joy in your favor! Lord, we have within us your memorial, received at your spiritual table; let us possess it in its full reality when all things shall be made new.

We glimpse the beauty that is laid up for us when we gaze upon the spiritual beauty your immortal will now creates within our mortal selves.

Savior, your crucifixion marked the end of your mortal life. Teach us to crucify ourselves and make way for our life in the Spirit. May your resurrection, Jesus, bring true greatness to our spiritual self and may your sacraments be the mirror wherein we may know that self.

Savior, your divine plan for the world is a mirror for the spiritual world. Teach us to walk in that world as spiritual persons.

Lord, do not deprive our souls of the spiritual vision of you nor our bodies of your warmth and sweetness. The mortality lurking in our bodies spreads corruption through us. May the spiritual waters of your love cleanse the effects of mortality from our hearts. Grant, Lord, that we may hasten to our true city and, like Moses on the mountaintop, possess it now in vision.

Sermon 3, 2.4–5: ed. Lamy 1, 216–222

JUNE 14

✠

Basil the Great
Bishop of Caesarea, 379

A reading from the treatise On the Holy Spirit, *written c. 375 by Basil the Great, Bishop of Caesarea, prior to the Second Ecumenical Council*

The communion of the Spirit with the Father and the Son may be understood by considering the creation of the angels. The pure, spiritual, and transcendent powers are called holy, because they have received holiness from the grace of the Holy Spirit. The historian has described for us only the creation of visible things and passes over the creation of the bodiless hosts in silence. But "from visible things we are able to construct analogies of invisible things, and so we glorify the Maker in whom all things were created, in heaven and on earth, visible and invisible," whether thrones or dominions or principalities or authorities, or any other reason-endowed nature whose name we do not know. When you consider creation I advise you first to think of Him who is the first cause of everything that exists: namely, the Father, and then of the Son, who is the creator, and then of the Holy Spirit, the perfector. So the ministering spirits exist by the will of the Father, are brought into being by the work of the Son, and are perfected by the presence of the Spirit, since angels are perfected by perseverance in holiness.

"The Originator of all things is One." He creates through the Son and perfects through the Spirit. The Father's work is in no way imperfect, since He accomplishes all in all, nor is the Son's work deficient if it is not completed by the Spirit. The Father creates through His will alone and does not "need" the Son, yet chooses to work through the Son. Likewise the Son works as the Father's likeness, and needs no other cooperation, but He chooses to have His work completed through the Spirit. "By the Word of the Lord the heavens were made, and all their host by the Spirit of His mouth."

On the Holy Spirit 38: PG 32, 135–136

JUNE 15

✠

Evelyn Underhill
Mystic, 1941

A reading of excerpts from the book Worship *by Evelyn Underhill, Mystic, published in 1936*

WORSHIP, in all its grades and kinds, is the response of the creature to the Eternal: nor need we limit this definition to the human sphere. There is a sense in which we may think of the whole life of the Universe, seen and unseen, conscious and unconscious, as an act of worship, glorifying its Origin, Sustainer, and End. Only in some such context, indeed, can we begin to understand the emergence and growth of the spirit of worship in men, or the influence which it exerts upon their concrete activities. Thus worship may be overt or direct, unconscious or conscious. Where conscious, its emotional colour can range from fear through reverence to self-oblivious love. But whatever its form of expression may be, it is always a subject-object relationship; and its general existence therefore constitutes a damaging criticism of all merely subjective and immanental explanations of Reality. For worship is an acknowledgment of Transcendence; that is to say, of a Reality independent of the worshipper, which is always more or less deeply coloured by mystery, and which is there first.

So, directly we take this strange thing Worship seriously, and give it the status it deserves among the various responses of men to their environment, we find that it obliges us to take up a particular attitude towards that environment. Even in its crudest form, the law of prayer—indeed the fact of prayer—is already the law of belief; since humanity's universal instinct to worship cannot be accounted for, if naturalism tells the whole truth about life. That

119

instinct means the latent recognition of a metaphysical reality, standing over against physical reality, which men are driven to adore, and long to apprehend. In other words it is the implicit, even though unrecognized Vision of God—that disclosure of the Supernatural which is overwhelming, self-giving, and attractive all at once—which is the first cause of all worship, from the puzzled upward glance of the primitive to the delighted self-oblation of the saint.

The worshipping life of the Christian, whilst profoundly personal, is essentially that of a person who is also a member of a group. In this, of course, it reproduces on spiritual levels the twofold character of his natural life; disciplined and supported by the social framework, to which each of its members has a personal responsibility and makes a personal contribution, but inwardly free. The Christian as such cannot fulfil his spiritual obligations in solitude. He forms part of a social and spiritual complex with a new relation to God; an organism which is quickened and united by that Spirit of supernatural charity which sanctifies the human race from above, and is required to incarnate something of this supernatural charity in the visible world. Therefore even his most lonely contemplations are not merely a private matter; but always to be regarded in their relation to the purpose and action of God Who incites them, and to the total life of the Church.

The Christian liturgy—taking this word now in its most general sense—is the artistic embodiment of this social yet personal life. Here we are not concerned with its historic origins, its doctrinal implications, or the chief forms it has assumed in the course of its development: but simply with its here-and-now existence, value, and meaning as the ordered framework of the Church's corporate worship, the classic medium by which the ceaseless adoring action of the Bride of Christ is given visible and audible expression. It is plain that the living experience of this whole Church, visible and invisible, past and present, stretched out in history and yet poised on God, must set the scene for Christian worship; not the poor little scrap of which any one soul, or any sectional group, is capable.

Edit. Harper and Brothers (N.Y., 1957), 3–4, 83, 85

J U N E 1 6

✠

Joseph Butler
Bishop of Durham, 1752

A reading from the conclusion of The Analogy of Religion *by Joseph Butler, Bishop of Durham, published in 1736*

Revelation claims to be the voice of God: and our obligation to attend to [this] voice is surely moral, in all cases. And as it is insisted, that its evidence is conclusive, upon thorough consideration of it; so it offers itself with obvious appearances of having something more than human in it, and therefore in all reason requires to have its claims most seriously examined into.

As to the particular method of our redemption, the appointment of a Mediator between God and man: this has been shown to be most obviously analogous to the general conduct of nature, *i.e.* the God of nature, in appointing others to be the instruments of his mercy, as we experience in the daily course of Providence. The condition of this world, which the doctrine of our redemption by Christ presupposes, so much falls in with natural appearances, that heathen moralists inferred it from those appearances: inferred that human nature was fallen from its original rectitude, and in consequence of this, degraded from its primitive happiness. However this opinion came into the world, these appearances kept up the tradition, and confirmed the belief of it. And as it was the general opinion under the light of nature, that repentance and reformation, alone and by itself, was not sufficient to do away sin, and procure a full remission of the penalties annexed to it; and as the reason of the thing does not at all lead to any such conclusion; so every day's experience shows us, that reformation is not, in any sort, sufficient to prevent the present disadvantages and miseries, which, in the natural course of things, God has annexed to folly and extravagance.

Yet there may be ground to think, that the punishments, which, by the general laws of divine government, are annexed to vice, may be prevented: that provision may have been, even originally, made, that they should be prevented by some means or other, though they could not by reformation alone. For we have daily instances of such mercy, in the general conduct of nature: compassion provided for misery, medicines for diseases, friends against enemies. There is provision made, in the original constitution of the world, that much of the natural bad consequences of our follies, which persons themselves alone cannot prevent, may be prevented by the assistance of others; assistance which nature enables, and disposes, and appoints them to afford. By a method of goodness analogous to this, when the world lay in wickedness, and consequently in ruin, "God so loved the world, that he gave his only-begotten Son to save it: and he being made perfect by suffering, became the author of eternal salvation to all them that obey him."

With regard to Christianity, it will be observed that there is a middle between a full satisfaction of the truth of it, and a satisfaction of the contrary. The middle state of mind between these two consists in a serious apprehension, that it may be true, joined with doubt whether it is so. And this, upon the best judgment I am able to make, is as far towards speculative infidelity, as any sceptic can at all be supposed to go, who has had true Christianity, with the proper evidences of it, laid before him, and has in any tolerable measure considered them. For I would not be mistaken to comprehend all who have ever heard of it; because it seems evident, that in many countries called Christian, neither Christianity nor its evidence, is fairly laid before men. And in places where both are, there appear to be some who have very little attended to either, and who reject Christianity with a scorn proportionate to their inattention; and yet are by no means without understanding in other matters. Now it has been shown, that a serious apprehension that Christianity may be true, lays persons under the strictest obligations of a serious regard to it, throughout the whole of their life; a regard not the same exactly, but in many respects nearly the same with what a full conviction of its truth would lay them under.

Joseph Butler. The Analogy of Religion, Natural and Revealed, to the Constitution and Course of Nature. Ed. Howard Malcom (Philadelphia, 1887), 307, 310–311, 313

JUNE 18

✠

Bernard Mizeki

Catechist and Martyr in Rhodesia, 1896

A reading from the recollections of John [Shoniwa] Kapuya concerning Bernard Mizeki, Catechist and Martyr in Rhodesia, 1896

I placed the goat on the ground, and was preparing to sacrifice it when I saw a man at the shallow ford washing his clothes.

"Who is that man?" I asked my mother.

"He is Bernard, the Umfundisi, the teacher who has come to live here. He is Mangwende's friend."

I said to my mother, "Mother, I wish to speak to the teacher."
She gave me her permission, and this was our conversation.

"Good morning, Umfundisi," I greeted him.

"Good morning," Bernard replied. "What is your name and from whence do you come?"

"My name is Shoniwa. I come from Demha, whom I have consulted because I am sick."

"What did she tell you and what did she do?"

"She cut my back and caught the blood in a horn. She rubbed in medicine and then her spirit told me that I must sacrifice a black goat, with no white hairs, to the spirit of Chigariro at this cascade. There is the goat, and here we are come, my mother and I, to do this thing."

"And what will that do for you?"

I told him then about the spirit of Chigariro, of his anger and desire for revenge, and of how his spirit had come against me to cause my sickness.

Bernard, the teacher, laughed and said, "It is all lies. It is not true."

"Lies, you say? But how can this be? What can I do?"

"Do not do what she tells you. It is not true."

"Umfundisi, do you not make sacrifices to the spirits?"

"No. I do not."

"But Umfundisi, how can you live without the protection of the good spirits against the bad spirits that would harm you?"

"No spirits can harm you, Shoniwa."

"Have you no spirits, Umfundisi, to keep you safe, to keep you from harm, to look after you and make you a strong man?"

"Yes, Shoniwa. I have a Spirit, the Spirit of God. It is the Holy Spirit."

When we reached the teacher's house, I said, "Please, Umfundisi, tell me more. Tell me, what is the work of God?"

"He loves us and gives us our food and shelter, the trees, the grass and the earth for our gardens."

"If I do not sacrifice the goat, will I live?"

"Yes, Shoniwa. You will live, if you pray."

"But I do not know how to pray."

"I shall teach you."

The teacher took a book, and told me words from the book and I believed them.

One night, Bernard, Chigwada, and I were sleeping in the same hut. We lay down on our mats, but I did not fall asleep. In the light from the fire, I saw Bernard rise and kneel down. He made a sign with his hand. He touched his forehead, then his breast, then his left shoulder and then his right shoulder—like this. Then for a long time, he remained silent with his eyes closed. He did not move. When he lay down on his mat once more, I rose and went to kneel where he had knelt. I said to myself, "Bernard, the teacher, has been praying, and if I wish to pray I must imitate him. This must be the special place where he hears the voice of God, so I must kneel here too, and do as he did." I too made the sign. Slowly I touched my forehead, my breast, my left shoulder, my right shoulder. I waited, I closed my eyes, I waited again, but nothing happened. Then I heard Chigwada laughing. He thought it was comical, and he jeered at me until Bernard sat up and was angry with him.

"Be quiet!" Bernard said in a strong voice. "Do not laugh."

He turned to me and said, "Do not be troubled, Shoniwa. That is the beginning of your first prayer to God. He will help you and I shall teach you."

Jean Farrant. Mashonaland Martyr: Bernard Mizeki and the Pioneer Church (London, 1966), 129–132

✠

Alban

First Martyr of Britain, c. 304

A reading from the Ecclesiastical History of England *by Bede the Venerable, Priest and Monk of Jarrow, concerning Alban, the Proto-Martyr of Britain*

When these unbelieving emperors were issuing savage edicts against all Christians, Alban, as yet a pagan, gave shelter to a Christian priest fleeing from his pursuers. And when he observed this person's unbroken activity of prayer and vigil, he was suddenly touched by the grace of God and began to follow the priest's example of faith and devotion. Gradually instructed by his teaching of salvation, Alban renounced the darkness of idolatry, and sincerely accepted Christ. But when the priest had lived in his house some days, word came to the ears of the evil ruler that Christ's confessor, whose place of martyrdom had not yet been appointed, lay hidden in Alban's house. Accordingly he gave orders to his soldiers to make a thorough search, and when they arrived at the martyr's house, holy Alban, wearing the priest's long cloak, at once surrendered himself in the place of his guest and teacher, and was led bound before the judge.

When Alban was brought in, the judge happened to be standing before an altar, offering sacrifice to devils. Seeing Alban, he was furious that he had presumed to put himself in such hazard by surrendering himself to the soldiers in place of his guest and ordered him to be dragged before the idols where he stood. "Since you have chosen to conceal a sacrilegious rebel," he said, "rather than surrender him to my soldiers to pay the well-deserved penalty for his blasphemy against our gods, you shall undergo all the tortures due to him if you dare to abandon the practice of our religion." But Saint Alban, who had freely confessed himself a Christian to the enemies of the faith, was unmoved by these threats, and armed with spiritual strength, openly refused to obey this order. "What is your family and race?" demanded the judge. "How does my family concern you?" replied Alban. "If you wish to know the truth about my religion, know that I am a Christian, and carry out Christian rites." "I demand to know your name," insisted the judge, "tell me at once." "My parents named me Alban," he answered, "and I worship and adore the living and true God, who created all things." The judge was very angry, and said: "If you want to enjoy eternal life, sacrifice at once to the great gods." Alban replied: "You are offering these sacrifices to devils, who cannot help their suppliants, nor answer their prayers and vows. On the contrary, whosoever offers sacrifice to idols is doomed to the pains of hell."

The soldier who had been moved by divine intuition to refuse to slay God's confessor was beheaded at the same time as Alban. And although he had not received the purification of Baptism, there was no doubt that he was cleansed by the shedding of his own blood, and rendered fit to enter the kingdom of heaven. Astonished by these many strange miracles, the judge called a halt to the persecution, and whereas he had formerly fought to crush devotion to Christ, he now began to honor the death of his saints.

Ecclesiastical History 1, 7: Colgrave and Mynors, 28–35

JUNE 28

✠

Irenaeus
Bishop of Lyons, c. 202

A reading from the treatise Against Heresies, *written in the late second century by Irenaeus, Bishop of Lyons*

Sacrifices, therefore, do not sanctify anyone, for God stands in no need of sacrifice; but it is the conscience of the offerer that sanctifies the sacrifice when it is pure and thus moves God to accept [the offering] as from a friend.

Inasmuch, then, as the church offers with single-mindedness, her gift is justly reckoned a pure sacrifice with God. As Paul also says to the Philippians: "I am filled, having received from Epaphroditus the things that were sent from you, a fragrant offering, a sacrifice acceptable and pleasing to God."

But how can they be consistent with themselves, [who say] that the bread over which thanks have been given is the body of their Lord, and the cup his blood, if they do not call Him the Son of the Creator of the world, that is, his Word, through whom the wood fructifies, and the fountains gush forth, and the earth gives "first the blade, then the ear, then the full corn in the ear."

Again, how can they say that the flesh, which is nourished with the body of the Lord and with his blood, goes to corruption, and does not partake of life? Let them, therefore, either alter their opinion, or cease from offering the things just mentioned. But our opinion is in accordance with the Eucharist, and the Eucharist in turn establishes our opinion.

Now we make offering to him, not as though he stood in need of it, but rendering thanks for his gift, and thus sanctifying what has been created. For even as God does not need our possessions, so we do need to offer something to God; as Solomon says: "He that has pity upon the poor, lends unto the Lord." For God, who stands in need of nothing, takes our good works to himself for this purpose, that he may grant us a recompense of his own good things; as our Lord says: "Come, you blessed of My Father, receive the kingdom prepared for you. For I was hungry, and you gave me to eat: I was thirsty, and you gave me drink: I was a stranger, and you took me in; naked, and you clothed me; sick, and you visited me; in prison, and you came to me."

Against Heresies 4, 18, 3–6: SC 100, 604–615

J U L Y 1 1

✠

Benedict of Nursia
Abbot of Monte Cassino, c. 540

A reading from the Prologue to the Rule of Saint Benedict *for monks, compiled around the year 540*

Listen, my son, to the precepts of the master and incline the ear of your heart. Freely accept and faithfully fulfill the advice of a loving father, that by the labor of obedience you may return to God from whom you have strayed by the sloth of disobedience. My words are addressed to all of you who, renouncing your own will in order to fight for the true sovereign Christ the Lord, take up the strong and glorious weapons of obedience.

First of all, whatever good work you undertake, ask God with most urgent prayer to accomplish it, so that he who has now willed to number us among his children may never be provoked by our evil behavior. For we must always so serve him with the gifts which he has bestowed on us that he may never as an angry father disinherit his children, nor yet as a dreaded lord be provoked by our sins to cast into eternal punishment the wicked servants who would not follow him to glory.

Let us then exert ourselves now. The Scripture awakens us, saying: "Now is the hour for us to rise from sleep," and with eyes open to the divine light and ears attentive to the word of God let us hear what his voice repeats to us every day: "Today if you will hear his voice, harden not your hearts." And again: "Those who have ears to hear, let them hear what the Spirit says to the churches." And what is said? "Come, my children, hearken unto me and I will teach you the fear of the Lord. Run while you have the light of life, that the darkness of death overtake you not."

We must, therefore, put on faith and the performance of good works, and led by the Gospel walk in his paths, so that we may deserve to see him who has called us into his kingdom. And, if we wish to dwell in the tabernacle of his kingdom, we must run toward it with good deeds or we shall not reach it. But let us ask the Lord with the prophet: "Lord, who shall dwell in your tabernacle, or who shall rest upon your holy mountain?" and listen as he answers and shows us the way to that dwelling-place: "Those who walk blamelessly and do what is right and speak the truth from their heart, who do not slander with their tongue and do no evil to their friends nor take reproach against their neighbors." It is they who take hold of the evil spirit that tempts us and cast him and his temptations out of the heart, thus frustrating him, those who seize evil suggestions as they arise and dash them on the rock that is Christ. It is they who fear the Lord without growing proud of virtue and humbly acknowledge that what is good does not proceed from themselves but from the Lord, who with the prophet bless the work of God in themselves: "Not unto us, Lord, not unto us, but unto your name give the glory."

Having answered us in full, the Lord expects that our works should daily correspond with these sacred instructions. Therefore, he has extended the days of our life and granted us a truce, in order to afford us an opportunity of making peace with him.

And so, after asking the Lord about the dwellers in his tabernacle and learning what is the duty of one who would dwell therein, it remains for us to fulfill these duties. For this reason, we must prepare our hearts and bodies to fight under the holy obedience of the Lord's commands, and ask God to give us the help of his grace where our nature is powerless. To escape the pains of hell and reach eternal life, we must, while there is still time, while we are in this body and can accomplish all these things by the light of this life, hasten to practice now the virtues that will profit us for eternity.

Therefore, we are going to establish a school of the Lord's service. In founding this we hope to introduce nothing harsh or burdensome. But if for some good reason, to amend evil habits or preserve charity, there be some strictness of discipline, do not immediately be dismayed and seek to flee from the way of salvation, whose entrance must necessarily be narrow. But, as we progress in this way of life and in faith, our hearts will expand and we will run the way of God's commandments with unspeakable delights of love. In this way, never quitting this rule but persevering in his teaching in the monastery until death, we will here share by patience in the sufferings of Christ, and deserve to be partakers also of his kingdom.

RB 1980: The Rule of St. Benedict in Latin and English with Notes, ed. Timothy Fry (Collegeville, 1981), 156–167

William White

Bishop of Pennsylvania, 1836

A reading from The Case of the Episcopal Churches Considered *by William White, Bishop of Pennsylvania, published in 1782*

The power of electing a superior order of ministers ought to be in the clergy and laity together, they being both interested in the choice. In England, the bishops are appointed by the civil authority; which was an usurpation of the crown at the Norman conquest, but since confirmed by acts of parliament. The primitive churches were generally supplied by popular elections; even in the city of Rome, the privilege of electing the bishop continued with the people to the tenth or eleventh century, and near those times there are resolves of councils, that none should be promoted to ecclesiastical dignities, but by election of the clergy and people. It cannot be denied that this right vested in numerous bodies, occasioned great disorders; which it is expected will be avoided, when the people shall exercise the right by representation.

Let us next take a view of the grounds on which the authority of episcopacy is asserted.

The advocates for this form maintain, that there having been an episcopal power originally lodged by Jesus Christ with his apostles, and by them exercised generally in person, but sometimes by delegation (as in the instances of Timothy and Titus) the same was conveyed by them before their decease to one pastor in each church, which generally comprehended all the Christians in a city and a convenient surrounding district. Thus were created the apostolic successors, who, on account of their settled residence are called bishops *by restraint;* whereas the apostles themselves were bishops *at large*, exercising episcopal power over all the churches, except in the case of St. James, who from the beginning was bishop of Jerusalem. From this time the word "episcopos," used in the New Testament indiscriminately with the word "presbuteros" (particularly in the 20th chapter of the Acts where the same persons are called "episcopoi" and "presbuteroi"), became *appropriated* to the superior order of ministers. That the apostles were thus succeeded by an order of ministers superior to pastors in general, episcopalians think they prove by the testimonies of the ancient fathers, and from the improbability that so great an innovation (as some conceive it) could have found general and peaceable possession in the 2d or 3d century, when episcopacy is on both sides acknowledged to have been prevalent. The argument is here concisely stated, but (as is believed) impartially.

The Case of the Episcopal Churches Considered, ed. Richard G. Salomon (Church Historical Society publication no. 39, 1954), 23–24, 36

JULY 24

✠

Thomas a Kempis
Priest, 1471

A reading from The Imitation of Christ, *published c. 1418 by Thomas a Kempis, Priest and ascetical writer*

"Whoever who follows me shall not walk in darkness," says Our Lord. In these words Christ counsels us to follow his life and way if we desire true enlightenment and freedom from all blindness of heart. Let the life of Jesus Christ, then, be our first consideration.

The teaching of Jesus far transcends all the teachings of the saints, and whosoever has his spirit will discover heavenly manna concealed within it. But many people, although they often hear the Gospel, feel little desire to follow it, because they lack the spirit of Christ. Whoever desires to understand and take delight in the words of Christ must strive to conform their whole life to him.

Of what use is it to discourse learnedly on the Trinity, if you lack humility and therefore displease the Trinity? Lofty words do not make a person just or holy; but a good life makes one dear to God. I would far rather feel contrition than be able to define it. If you knew the whole Bible by heart, and all the teachings of the philosophers, how would this help you without the grace and love of God? "Vanity of vanities, and all is vanity," except to love God and serve him alone. And this is supreme wisdom: to despise the world, and draw daily nearer the kingdom of heaven.

It is vanity to solicit honors, or to raise oneself to high station. It is vanity to be a slave to bodily desires, and to crave for things which bring certain retribution. It is vanity to wish for long life, if you care little for a good life. It is vanity to give thought only to this present life, and to care nothing for the life to come. It is vanity to love things that so swiftly pass away, and not to hasten onwards to that place where everlasting joy abides.

Keep constantly in mind the saying: "The eye is not satisfied with seeing, nor the ear filled with hearing." Strive to withdraw your heart from the love of visible things, and direct your affections to things invisible. For those who follow only their natural inclinations defile their conscience, and lose the grace of God.

The Imitation of Christ 1, 1

JULY 26

✠

The Parents of the Blessed Virgin Mary

A reading from a sermon of John of Damascus, Priest, concerning Joachim and Anne, the parents of the Blessed Virgin Mary

Anne was to be the mother of the Virgin Mother of God, and hence nature did not dare to anticipate the flowering of grace. Thus nature remained sterile, until grace produced its fruit. For she who was to be born had to be a first-born daughter, since she would be the mother of the first-born of all creation, "in whom all things are held together."

Joachim and Anne, how blessed a couple! All creation is indebted to you. For at your hands the creator was offered a gift excelling all other gifts: a chaste mother, who alone was worthy of the creator.

And so rejoice, Anne, that "you were sterile and have not borne children; break forth into shouts, you who have not given birth." Rejoice, Joachim, because from your daughter "a child is born for us, a Son is given us, whose name is messenger of great counsel and universal salvation, mighty God." For this child is God.

Joachim and Anne, how blessed and spotless a couple! You will be known by the fruit you have borne, as the Lord says: "By their fruits you will know them." The conduct of your life pleased God and was worthy of your daughter. For by the chaste and holy life you led together, you have fashioned a jewel of virginity: she who remained a virgin before, during and after giving birth. She alone for all time would maintain her virginity in mind and soul as well as in body.

Joachim and Anne, how chaste a couple! While safeguarding the chastity prescribed by the law of nature, you achieved with God's help something which transcends nature in giving the world the

Virgin Mother of God as your daughter. While leading a devout and holy life in your human nature, you gave birth to a daughter nobler than the angels, whose queen she now is. Girl of utter beauty and delight, daughter of Adam and mother of God, blessed are the loins and blessed the womb from which you come! Blessed the arms that carried you, and blessed are your parents' lips. "Rejoice in God, all the earth. Sing, exult and sing hymns." Raise your voice, raise it and be not afraid.

Oration 6 on the Nativity of the Blessed Virgin Mary 2, 4, 5, 6: PG 96, 663, 667, 670

JULY 27

✠

William Reed Huntington
Priest, 1909

A reading from The Church-Idea *by William Reed Huntington, Priest, published in 1870*

What are the essential, the absolutely essential features of the Anglican position? When it is proposed to make Anglicanism the basis of a Church of the Reconciliation, it is above all things necessary to determine what Anglicanism pure and simple is. The word brings up before the eyes of some a flutter of surplices, a vision of village spires and cathedral towers, a somewhat stiff and stately company of deans, prebendaries, and choristers, and that is about all. But we greatly mistake if we imagine that the Anglican principle has no substantial existence apart from these accessories. Indeed, it is only when we have stripped Anglicanism of the picturesque costume which English life has thrown around it, that we can fairly study its anatomy, or understand its possibilities of power and adaptation.

The Anglican *principle* and the Anglican *system* are two very different things. The writer does not favor attempting to foist the whole Anglican system upon America; while yet he believes that the Anglican principle is America's best hope.

At no time since the Reformation has the Church of England been in actual fact the spiritual home of the nation. A majority of the people of Great Britain are to-day without her pale. Could a system which has failed to secure comprehensiveness on its native soil, hope for any larger measure of success in a strange land?

But what if it can be shown that the Anglican system has failed in just so far as it has been untrue to the Anglican principle? And what if it can be shown that here in America we have an opportunity to give that principle the only fair trial it has ever had?

The true Anglican position, like the City of God in the Apocalypse, may be said to lie foursquare. Honestly to accept that position is to accept,—

1st. The Holy Scriptures as the Word of God.

2d. The Primitive Creeds as the Rule of Faith.

3d. The two Sacraments ordained by Christ himself.

4th. The Episcopate as the key-stone of Governmental Unity.

These four points, like the four famous fortresses of Lombardy, make "the Quadrilateral" of pure Anglicanism. Within them the Church of the Reconciliation may stand secure. Because the English State-Church has muffled these first principles in a cloud of non-essentials, and has said to the people of the land, "Take all this or nothing," she mourns today the loss of half her children. Only by avoiding the like fatal error can the American branch of the Anglican Church hope to save herself from becoming in effect, whatever she may be in name, a sect. Only by a wise discrimination between what can and what cannot be conceded for the sake of unity, is unity attainable.

If our whole ambition as Anglicans in America be to continue a small, but eminently respectable body of Christians, and to offer a refuge to people of refinement and sensibility, who are shocked by the irreverences they are apt to encounter elsewhere; in a word, if we care to be only a countercheck and not a force in society; then let us say as much in plain terms, and frankly renounce any and all claim to Catholicity. We have only, in such a case, to wrap the robe of our dignity about us, and walk quietly along in a seclusion no one will take much trouble to disturb. Thus may we be a Church in name, and a sect in deed.

But if we aim at something nobler that this, if we would have our Communion become national in very truth,—in other words, if we would bring the Church of Christ into the closest possible sympathy with the throbbing, sorrowing, sinning, repenting, aspiring heart of this great people,—then let us press our reasonable claims to be the reconciler of a divided household, not in a spirit of arrogance (which ill befits those whose best possessions have come to them by inheritance), but with affectionate earnestness and an intelligent zeal.

The Church-Idea (N.Y., 1870), 155–157, 210–211

JULY 29

✠

Mary and Martha of Bethany

A reading from a sermon of Augustine, Bishop of Hippo, concerning Mary and Martha of Bethany

Our Lord's words teach us that though we labor among the many distractions of this world, we should have only one goal. For we are but travelers on a journey without as yet a fixed abode; we are on our way, not yet in our native land; we are in a state of longing, but not yet of enjoyment. Let us continue on our way, and continue without sloth or respite, so that we may ultimately arrive at our destination.

Martha and Mary were sisters, related not only by blood but also by religious aspirations. They stayed close to our Lord and both served him harmoniously when he was among them. Martha welcomed him as a traveler is welcomed. But in her case, the maidservant received her Lord, the invalid her Savior, the creature her Creator, to serve him bodily food while she was to be fed by the Spirit. For the Lord willed to put on the form of a slave, and under this form to be fed by his own servants, out of condescension and not out of need. For this was indeed condescension, to present himself to be fed; since he was in the flesh he would in fact be hungry and thirsty.

You, Martha, if I may say so, are blessed for your good service, and for your labors you seek the reward of peace. Now you are much occupied in nourishing the body, admittedly a holy one. But when you come to the heavenly homeland will you find a traveler to welcome, someone hungry to feed, someone thirsty to whom you may give drink, someone ill whom you could visit, or quarreling whom you could reconcile, or dead whom you could bury?

139

No, there will be none of these tasks there. What you will find there is what Mary chose. There we shall not feed others, but we ourselves shall be fed. Thus what Mary chose in this life will be realized there in all its fullness. She was gathering fragments from that rich banquet, the Word of God. Do you wish to know what we will have there? The Lord himself tells us when he says of his servants: "Amen, I say to you, he will make them recline and passing he will serve them."

Sermon 103, 1–2, 6: PL 38, 613, 615

J U L Y   3 0

✠

William Wilberforce
Social Reformer and Member of Parliament, 1833

A reading from a Practical View of the Prevailing Religious System of Professed Christians, *published in 1797 by William Wilberforce, social reformer and Member of Parliament*

It may be proper to point out the very inadequate conception which [the bulk of professed Christians] entertain of the importance of Christianity in general, of its peculiar nature, and superior excellence. If we listen to their conversation, virtue is praised, and vice is censured; piety is perhaps applauded, and profaneness condemned. So far all is well. But let any one, who would not be deceived by these barren generalities, examine a little more closely, and he will find, that not to Christianity in particular, but at best to religion in general, perhaps to mere morality, their homage is intended to be paid. With Christianity, as distinct from these, they are little acquainted; their views of it have been so cursory and superficial, that far from discerning its peculiar characteristics, they have little more than perceived those exterior circumstances which distinguish it from other forms of religion. There are some few facts, and perhaps some leading doctrines and principles, of which they cannot be wholly ignorant; but of the consequences and relations, and practical uses of these, they have few ideas, or none at all.

Does this language seem too strong? View their plan of life and their ordinary conduct; and let us ask, wherein can we discern the points of discrimination between them and professed unbelievers? In an age wherein it is confessed and lamented that infidelity abounds, do we observe in them any remarkable care to instruct their children in the principles of the faith which they profess, and to furnish them with arguments for the defence of it? They would blush, on their child's coming out into the world, to think him defective in the branch of that knowledge, or of those accomplishments, which belong to his station in life; and, accordingly, these are cultivated with becoming assiduity. But he is left to collect his religion as he may: the study of Christianity has formed no part of his education; and his attachment to it, where any attachment to it exists at all, is too often, not the preference of sober reason and conviction, but merely the result of early and groundless prepossession. He was born in a Christian country; of course he is a Christian:—his father was a member of the Church of England; so is he. When such is the religion handed down among us by hereditary succession, it cannot surprise us to observe young men of sense and spirit beginning to doubt altogether of the truth of the system in which they have been brought up, and ready to abandon a station which they are unable to defend. Knowing Christianity chiefly in the difficulties which it contains, and in the impossibilities which are falsely imputed to it, they fall, perhaps, into the company of infidels; where they are shaken by frivolous objections and profane cavils, which, had their religious persuasion been grounded in reason and argument, would have passed by them as the idle wind.

Let us beware before it be too late.

Edit. SCM Press (London, 1958), 11–12

JULY 31

✣

Joseph of Arimathaea

A reading about Joseph of Arimathaea from the Apocryphal Gospel of Nicodemus, *also called the* Acts of Pilate

They said to Joseph: "We were very angry because you asked for the body of Jesus, and wrapped it in a clean linen cloth, and placed it in a tomb. And for this reason we secured you in a house with no window, and locked and sealed the door, and guards watched where you were shut up. And on the first day of the week we opened it, and did not find you, and were much troubled, and all the people of God were amazed until yesterday. And now tell us what happened to you."

And Joseph said: "On the day of preparation about the tenth hour you shut me in, and I remained the whole sabbath. And at midnight as I stood and prayed, the house where you shut me in was raised up by the four corners, and I saw as it were a lightning flash in my eyes. Full of fear I fell to the ground, and someone took me by the hand and raised me up from the place where I had fallen, and something moist like water flowed from my head to my feet, and the smell of fragrant oil reached my nostrils. And he wiped my face and kissed me and said to me: Do not fear, Joseph. Open your eyes and see who it is who speaks with you. I looked up and saw Jesus. Trembling, I thought it was a phantom, and I said the (ten) commandments. And he said them with me. Now as you well know, a phantom immediately flees if it meets anyone and hears the commandments. And when I saw that he said them with me, I said to him: Rabbi Elijah! He said: I am not Elijah.

"And I said to him: Who are you, Lord? He replied: I am Jesus, whose body you asked for from Pilate, whom you clothed in clean linen, on whose face you placed a cloth, and whom you placed in your new cave, and you rolled a great stone to the door of the cave. And I asked him who spoke to me: Show me the place where I laid you. And he took me and showed me the place where I laid him. And the linen cloth lay there, and the cloth that was upon his face. Then I recognised that it was Jesus."

Acts of Pilate 15, 5–6: New Testament Apocrypha, ed. Wilhelm Schneemelcher and transl. R. McL. Wilson (revised edition, vol. 1, Cambridge, 1991), 518; cf. C. Tischendorf. Evangelia Apocrypha (Leipzig, 1853), 250–251

AUGUST 7

✠

John Mason Neale
Priest, 1866

A reading from an essay on English Hymnology: Its History and Prospects, *published in 1849 by John Mason Neale, Priest and hymnographer*

AMONG the most pressing of the inconveniences consequent on the adoption of the vernacular language in the office-books of the Reformation, must be reckoned the immediate disuse of all the hymns of the Western Church. That treasury, into which the saints of every age and country had poured their contributions, delighting, each in his generation, to express their hopes and fears, their joys and sorrows, in language which should be the heritage of their Holy Mother to the end of time—those noble hymns, which had solaced anchorets on their mountains, monks in their cells, priests in bearing up against the burden and heat of the day, missionaries in girding themselves for martyrdom—henceforth they became as a sealed book and as a dead letter. The prayers and collects, the versicles and responses, of the earlier Church might, without any great loss of beauty, be preserved; but the hymns, whether of the sevenfold daily office, of the weekly commemoration of creation and redemption, of the yearly revolution of the Church's seasons, or of the birthdays to glory of martyrs and confessors—those hymns by which day unto day had uttered speech, and night unto night had taught knowledge—they could not, by the hands then employed in ecclesiastical matters, be rendered into another, and that a then comparatively barbarous, tongue. One attempt the Reformers made—the version of the *Veni Creator Spiritus* in the Ordinal; and that, so far perhaps fortunately, was the only one. Cranmer, indeed, expressed some casual hope that men fit for the office might be induced to come forward; but the very idea of a hymnology of the time of Henry VIII may make us feel thankful that the primate's wish was not carried out.

The Church of England had, then, to wait. She had, as it has been well said, to begin over again. There might arise saints within herself, who, one by one, should enrich her with hymns in her own language; there might arise poets, who should be capable of supplying her office-books with versions of the hymns of earlier times.

In the meantime the psalms were her own; and grievous as was the loss she had sustained, she might be content to suffice herself with those, and expect in patience the rest.

The Christian Remembrancer 18 (July–December 1849), 303–304

AUGUST 8

✠

Dominic

Priest and Friar, 1221

A reading from various writings on the history of the Order of Preachers concerning Dominic, Priest and Friar, their Founder, who died in 1221

Dominic possessed such great integrity and was so strongly motivated by divine love, that without a doubt he proved to be a bearer of honor and grace. He was a man of great serenity, except when moved to compassion and mercy. And since a joyful heart animates the face, he displayed the peaceful composure of a spiritual person in the kindness he manifested outwardly and by the cheerfulness of his countenance.

Wherever he went he showed himself in word and deed to be a follower of the Gospel. During the day no one was more community-minded or pleasant toward associates. During the night hours no one was more persistent in every kind of vigil and supplication. Dominic seldom spoke unless it was with God, that is, in prayer, or about God; and in this matter he instructed his brothers.

Frequently Dominic made a special personal petition that

God would deign to grant him a genuine charity, effective in caring for and in obtaining the salvation of humankind. For he believed that only then would he be truly a member of Christ, when he had given himself totally for the salvation of all, just as the Lord Jesus, the Savior of all, had offered himself completely for our salvation. So, for this work, after a lengthy period of careful and provident planning, Dominic founded the Order of Friars Preachers.

In his conversations and letters he often urged the brothers of the Order to study constantly the Old and New Testaments. He always carried with him the gospel according to Matthew and the epistles of Paul, and so well did he study them that he almost knew them from memory. Two or three times Dominic was chosen bishop, but always refused, preferring to live with his brothers in poverty.

Libellus de Principiis OP: Acta canonizationis Sancti Dominici: Monumenta OP Mist. 16, Rome 1935, pp. 30ss, 146–147

AUGUST 10

✠

Laurence

Deacon, and Martyr at Rome, 258

A reading from a sermon of Leo the Great, Bishop of Rome, concerning Laurence the Deacon, who was martyred at Rome in the year 258 under the persecution of the emperor Valerian

August 10

When the fury of the heathen was raging against Christ's most chosen members and attacking those especially who were of priestly rank, the wicked persecutor's wrath was vented on Laurence the deacon, who was pre-eminent not only in the performance of the sacred rites but also in the management of the church's property. The persecutor promised himself double spoil from this person's capture; for if he forced him to surrender the sacred treasures, he would also drive him outside the boundaries of true religion.

Hence, this persecutor, so greedy of money and such a foe to the truth, armed himself with a double weapon: with avarice to plunder the gold, and with impiety to carry off Christ. He demanded that the church's wealth, on which his greedy mind was set, should be brought to him. But the holy deacon showed him where he had it stored by pointing to the multitudes of holy poor, in the feeding and clothing of whom he had a treasury of riches which could not be lost, and which were the more entirely safe because the money had been spent on so holy a cause.

The baffled plunderer, therefore, blazing out into hatred for a religion which had put riches to such a use, determined to pillage a still greater treasure by carrying off that sacred deposit wherewith he was enriched, since he could find no solid hoard of money in possession. He ordered Laurence to renounce Christ, and prepared to ply the deacon's stout courage with frightful tortures. The deacon's limbs, torn and mangled by many cutting blows, were commanded to be broiled upon the fire in an iron framework, which was of itself already hot enough to burn him, and on which his limbs were turned from time to time to make the torment fiercer and the death more lingering.

O raging cruelty, when Laurence departs for heaven, you are vanquished! The flame of Christ's love could not be overcome by your flames, and the fire which burnt outside was less keen than the one burning within.

Let us rejoice, then, with spiritual joy, and make our boast over the happy end of this illustrious servant of the Lord, who is "wonderful in all his saints."

Sermon 85, 2–4: PL 54, 435–437

AUGUST 11

✠

Clare

Abbess at Assisi, 1253

A reading from the proclamation of Pope Alexander IV in 1255 canonizing Clare, Abbess at Assisi and foundress of the Poor Clares, the second order of St. Francis

Clare collected all that she had and devoted it to the service of Christ in alms, changing everything into what might serve as gifts for the poor. In her flight from the world's clamor she went first to a church in the fields, and there received the holy tonsure from the blessed Francis himself. She then went on to another church, from whence her family tried to drag her away, but she took hold of the altar cloth and held on to it, in such a way that her relatives could see the [tonsure] cut in her hair. She offered a determined and continued resistance, on the ground that in the integrity of her mind she was joined to God already and could not be drawn away from his service. In the end, after she had been taken by the same blessed Francis to the church of San Damiano outside the city of Assisi, the place from which she came, the Lord added many companions to her in the love and service of his name.

Léopold de Chérance. St. Clare of Assisi (London, 1927), 231

AUGUST 13

✠

Jeremy Taylor

Bishop of Down, Connor, and Dromore, 1667

A reading from a Letter to a Gentlewoman Seduced to the Church of Rome, *written by Jeremy Taylor in 1657*

For its Doctrine, [the Church of England] is certain it professes the belief of all that is written in the Old and New Testament, all that which is in the three creeds, the Apostolical, the Nicene, and that of Athanasius, and whatsoever was decreed in the four general councils or in any other truly such; and whatsoever was condemned in these our church hath legally declared to be heresy. And upon these accounts above four whole ages of the church went to heaven; they baptized all their catechumens into this faith, their hopes of heaven were upon this and a good life, their saints and martyrs lived and died in this alone, they denied communion to none that professed this faith. "This is the catholic faith," so saith the creed of Athanasius; and unless a company of men have power to alter the faith of God, whosoever live and die in this faith are entirely catholic and Christian. So the Church of England hath the same faith without dispute that the church had for four or five hundred years, and therefore there could be nothing wanting here to saving faith if we live according to our belief.

And after this, what can be supposed wanting [in the Church of England] in order to salvation? We have the Word of God, the faith of the apostles, the creeds of the primitive church, the articles of the four first general councils, a holy liturgy, excellent prayers, perfect sacraments, faith and repentance, the ten commandments, and the sermons of Christ, and all the precepts and counsels of the Gospel. We teach the necessity of good works, and require and strictly exact the severity of a holy life. We live in obedience to God, and are ready to die for him, and do so when he requires us so to do. We speak honourably of his most Holy Name. We worship him at the mention of his Name. We confess his attributes. We love his servants. We pray for all men. We love all Christians, even our most erring brethren. We confess our sins to God and to our brethren whom we have offended, and to God's ministers in cases of scandal or of a troubled conscience. We communicate often. We are enjoined to receive the Holy Sacrament thrice every year at least. Our priests absolve the penitent. Our Bishops ordain priests, and confirm baptized persons, and bless their people and intercede for them. And what could here be wanting to salvation?

The Whole Works of the Rt. Rev. Jeremy Taylor, ed. R. Heber, rev. C.P. Eden, vol. 6 (London, 1852), 646–647

AUGUST 14

✠

Jonathan Myrick Daniels
Seminarian and Witness for Civil Rights, 1965

A reading from an account of his work in Selma, Alabama, by Jonathan Myrick Daniels, Seminarian and Witness for Civil Rights, written in April of 1965

There are good men here, just as there are bad men. There are competent leaders and a bungler here and there. We have activists who risk their lives to confront a people with the challenge of freedom and a nation with its conscience. We have neutralists who cautiously seek to calm troubled waters. We have men about the work of reconciliation who are willing to reflect upon the cost and pay it. Perhaps at one time or another [we] are all of these. Sometimes we take to the streets, sometimes we yawn through interminable meetings. Sometimes we talked with white men in their homes and offices, sometimes we sit out a murderous night with an alcoholic and his family because we love them and cannot stand apart. Sometimes we confront the posse, and sometimes we hold a child. Sometimes we stand with men who have learned to hate, and sometimes we must stand a little apart from them. Our life in Selma is filled with ambiguity, and in that we share with men everywhere. We are beginning to see as we never saw before that we are truly in the world and yet ultimately not of it. For through the bramble bush of doubt and fear and supposed success we are groping our way to the realization that above all else, we are called to be saints. That is the mission of the Church everywhere. And in this Selma, Alabama is like all the world: it needs the life and witness of militant *saints.*

"A Burning Bush," The New Hampshire Churchman 17:9 (June 1965); American Martyr: The Jon Daniels Story, ed. William J. Schneider (Harrisburg, Pa., 1992), 91

AUGUST 18

✠

William Porcher DuBose
Priest, 1918

A reading from the treatise High Priesthood and Sacrifice *by William Porcher DuBose, Priest, published in 1908*

August 18

WE have our religion through the medium of languages that have been long dead, and that present tendencies in education threaten to render more and more dead to us. Along with the languages, there is a growing disposition to relegate the ideas, the entire symbolic expression and form, of Christianity to the past. The modern world calls for modern modes of thought and modern forms of speech. We have to meet that demand and be able to answer and satisfy whatever of reason or truth there is in it.

Revelation, if it was to come at all, had to come at a time, and in the ideas and language of the time. All that was possible in mitigation of that inevitable disadvantage was that it should come at the best time;—and the best time would be the one whose ideas and language would be, not only the most universal possible in themselves, but also the most convertible into the thought and speech of all other times. From the Hebrew into the Greek, and thence into all succeeding forms of knowledge and expression among men—that, in all the long history of things as they have been, was the actual, as it cannot but seem to us the best, mode for the entrance of the things of God into the affairs of the world.

The time will never come when the Christian Church can surrender or neglect the Hebrew and Greek sources of its inspiration and life. And the world itself will be the richer and better if it will help us not to do so; if in all the channels and courses of higher education it will multiply the facilities and help us to magnify the importance of these best means to its own highest culture. There are two tasks before us as students and teachers of Christianity. The first is to know and understand our sources. To begin with, we must know our Old Testament as we have never known it before, if we are to take part in the new interpretation of our New Testament that the times demand. For each time must have its own living interpretation, since the interpretation cannot but be, in half measure at least, relative to the time. If the divine part in it is fixed, the human is progressive and changing just in so far as it is living.

All science of life now is a science of beginnings and of growth, or of evolution. The New Testament as absolutely transcends the Old as it fulfils it; but on the other hand, it is as actually the culmination and completion of the Old Testament as it transcends it. The thought, the language, the life of Christianity are from the very beginning Hebrew, transformed and as far as possible universalized by transition through Greek thought and speech. All this history has its meaning, and enters largely into the meaning and form of Christianity as we have it. But it brings with it also its embarrassments. The most immediate consequence comes to us in the manifest fact that we are attempting to address the world to-day, in the matter of its profoundest interest, in terms of the world two thousand years ago. We have first to know what those terms meant then, and to prove that all they meant then they mean now, and mean for all men in time. Are our Bible and our Creeds to be recognized by us as antiquated? Are the Hebrew phrases and terms of priesthood and sacrifice, and the Greek or Gentile application of them to the Cross of Christ, waxed old and ready to vanish away? Forever no!—but if not, then we must take measures to preserve them, and the only way to preserve them is to make them as living to-day, as much part of our thought and our speech and our life now, as they were two thousand years ago.

In order to do that, we must cease to treat the phraseology, the forms, definitions, and dogmas of Christianity as sacred relics, too sacred to be handled. We must take them out of their napkins, strip them of their cerements, and turn them into current coin. We must let them do business in the life that is living now, and take part in the thought and feeling and activity of the men of the world of to-day.

High Priesthood and Sacrifice (N.Y., 1908), 1–3

✠

Bernard

Abbot of Clairvaux, 1153

A reading from the treatise On the Love of God *by Bernard, Abbot of Clairvaux in the mid-twelfth century*

The cause of our loving God is God, for he is both origin of our love and its final goal. He is himself the occasion of human love; he also gives the power to love and brings desire to its consummation. In his essential being he is himself the Lovable One, and he provides himself as the object of our love. He desires that our love for him result in our happiness, not that it be empty and void. His love both opens up the way for our love and is our love's reward. How kindly does he lead us in love's way, how generously he returns the love we give, how sweet is he to those who wait for him! He is rich to all who call upon him, for he can give them nothing better than himself. He gave himself to be our Righteousness, and he keeps himself to be our great Reward. He sets himself to the refreshment of our souls and spends himself to free the prisoners.

You are good, Lord, to the soul that seeks you. What, then, are you to the soul that finds you? The marvel is, no one can seek you who has not found you already. You desire us to find so that we may seek, to seek so that we may find. We can both seek you and find you, but we can never anticipate you, for though we say, "Early shall my prayer come before you," a chilly, loveless thing would that prayer be, were it not warmed by your own breath and born of your own Spirit.

On the Love of God VII: 22; transl. Philip H. Pfatteicher. Festivals and Commemorations: Handbook to the Calendar in Lutheran Book of Worship (Minneapolis, 1980), 329; based on a translation by "A Religious of C.S.M.V." (1950) included in the Library of Christian Classics XIII, Late Medieval Mysticism ed. Ray C. Petry (Philadelphia, n.d.), 59–60.

✠

Louis

King of France, 1270

A reading from the Spiritual Testament to his Son *by Louis, King of France, who died in 1270*

My dearest son, my first instruction is that you should love the Lord your God with all your heart and all your strength. Without this there is no salvation. Keep yourself from everything that you know displeases God, that is to say, from every mortal sin. You should permit yourself to be tormented by every kind of martyrdom before you would allow yourself to commit a mortal sin.

If the Lord has permitted you to have some trial, bear it willingly and with gratitude, considering that it has happened for your good and that perhaps you well deserved it. If the Lord bestows upon you any kind of prosperity, thank him humbly and see that you become no worse for it, either through vain pride or anything else, because you ought not to oppose God or offend him in the matter of such gifts.

Listen to the divine office with pleasure and devotion. Whenever you are in church, be careful not to let your eyes wander and not to speak empty words, but pray to the Lord devoutly, either aloud or with the interior prayer of the heart.

Be kindhearted to the poor, the unfortunate and the afflicted. Give them as much help and consolation as you can. Thank God for all the benefits he has bestowed upon you, that you may be worthy to receive greater. Be just to your subjects, swaying neither to right nor left, but holding the line of justice. Always side with the poor rather than with the rich, until you are certain of the truth. See that all your subjects live in justice and peace, but especially those who have ecclesiastical rank and who belong to religious orders.

In conclusion, may the three persons of the Holy Trinity and all the saints protect you from every evil. And may the Lord give you the grace to do his will so that he may be served and honored through you, that in the next life we may together come to see him, love him, and praise him unceasingly.

Acta Sanctorum, August 5 (1868), 546

AUGUST 27

✠

Thomas Gallaudet, 1902 and Henry Winter Syle, 1890

Priests

A reading from the writings of Thomas Gallaudet, Priest and Apostle to the Deaf, published in 1853 and 1877

[*From an address in 1853:*]

At length the idea forced itself upon my mind that I ought to attempt to gather these persons around me in pastoral relations, and to establish for them a church. This idea gained strength from time to time, and having obtained the unanimous consent of the rectors of the different Episcopal churches in this city, I commenced holding the regular services of our church on the first Sunday of October, 1852, in this room in which we are now assembled. I have the morning service with the voice, that the parents, children, other relatives and friends of deaf-mutes may have the opportunity of joining with them in forming one parish. The afternoon I devote to the deaf-mutes, translating to them our service and preaching the same sermon which I use in the forenoon. The deaf-mutes have apparently taken great interest in this service, and have been present several times to the number of seventy and eighty.

[And from "A Sketch of My Life" for the year 1877:]

During the 25 years of our parish life there were 1,294 persons baptized and 913 confirmed. The names of 1,275 communicants were placed on our list. There were 587 marriages and 761 burials. A large proportion of each classification were deaf-mutes and their relatives. There were received about $36,850 for charitable work in the parish, $16,645 for objects outside of the parish and $238,000 for the support of the Church, buying its property and paying for its improvements and repairs. . . . For several years much earnest work has been done for the sick and needy in our midst. In our chapel, besides the Sunday Schools, there have been a day-school, a sewing-school, a mothers'-meeting, and a social week-night gathering. All this has finally crystallized into our Sisterhood and Brotherhood.

Otto B. Berg and Henry L. Buzzard. Thomas Gallaudet, Apostle to the Deaf (N.Y., 1989), 42, 53–54

AUGUST 28

✠

Augustine
Bishop of Hippo, 430

A reading from The City of God *by Augustine, Bishop of Hippo, written in the early fifth century after the fall of Rome in 410*

The whole earth sings a new song to the Lord, as was truly predicted in the Scriptures and in the writings of the prophets, where we read: "Sing to the Lord a new song; sing to the Lord, all the earth." And the title of this psalm is: "When the house was being built, after the captivity." Indeed this house, the City of God, which is the holy Church, is now being built to the Lord in all the earth after that captivity in which the demons held captive those persons who through faith in God became like the living stones of which the house is being built. For the fact that human beings were the makers of their gods did not mean that they were not held captive by the gods they had made, for by worshipping these gods they were drawn into fellowship with them, and I do not mean fellowship with senseless idols, but with cunning demons.

It is nothing but folly, nothing but miserable error, to humble yourself before a being you would hate to resemble in the conduct of your life, and to worship one whom you would refuse to imitate. For surely, the supremely important thing in religion is to model oneself on the object of one's worship.

City of God 8, 24 and 17: CCL 47, 243–244, 235

AUGUST 31

✠

Aidan

Bishop of Lindisfarne, 651

A reading from the Ecclesiastical History of England *by Bede the Venerable, Priest and Monk of Jarrow, concerning Aidan, first Bishop of Lindisfarne, in the seventh century*

On Aidan's arrival, the king appointed the island of Lindisfarne to be his see at his own request. As the tide ebbs and flows, this place is surrounded by sea twice a day like an island, and twice a day the sand dries and joins it to the mainland. The king always listened humbly and readily to Aidan's advice and diligently set himself to establish and extend the church of Christ throughout the kingdom. And while the bishop, who was not fluent in the English language, preached the Gospel, it was most delightful to see the king himself interpreting the word of God to his ealdorman and thanes.

It was from this island and from this community of monks that Aidan was sent, when he had been made bishop, to preach the faith of Christ to a province of the English. Among other evidences of holy life, he gave his clergy an inspiring example of self-discipline and continence, and the highest recommendation of his teaching to all was that he and his followers lived as they taught. Aidan never sought or cared for any worldly possessions, and loved to give away to the poor who chanced to meet him whatever he received from kings or wealthy folk. Whether in town or country, he always traveled on foot unless compelled by necessity to ride. Whatever people he met on his walks, whether high or low, he stopped and spoke to them. If they were heathen, he urged them to be baptized. If they were Christians, he strengthened their faith and inspired them by word and deed to live a good life and to be generous to others.

His life is in marked contrast to the apathy of our own times, for all who walked with him, whether monks or layfolk, were required to meditate, that is, either to read the Scriptures or to learn the psalms.

Nor would Aidan offer money to influential people, although he offered them food whenever he entertained them as host. But if the wealthy ever gave him gifts of money, he either distributed it for the needs of the poor, as I have mentioned, or else used it to ransom any who had unjustly been sold as slaves. Many of those whom he had ransomed in this way later became his disciples; and when they had been instructed and trained, he ordained them to the priesthood.

Ecclesiastical History 3, 3, 5: Colgrave and Mynors, 218–221, 226–229

SEPTEMBER 1

✠

David Pendleton Oakerhater
Deacon and Missionary of the Cheyenne, 1931

A reading from the first address to the assembled leaders of the Cheyenne nation, spoken by David Pendleton Oakerhater shortly after his ordination to the Diaconate in 1881, as recorded by John B. Wicks

You all know me. You remember when I led you out to war I went first, and what I told you was true. Now I have been away to the East and I have learned about another captain, the Lord Jesus Christ, and he is my leader. He goes first, and all he tells me is true. I come back to my people to tell you to go with me now in this new road, a war that makes all for peace and where we have only victory.

David Pendleton O-Kuh-Ha-Tah: God's Warrior, by Lois Clark (Oklahoma City, 1985), i; Owanah Anderson. Jamestown Commitment: The Episcopal Church and the American Indian (Cincinnati, 1988), 80; Alvin O. Turner, "Journey to Sainthood," in The Chronicles of Oklahoma LXX: 2 (Summer 1992), 132–133

S E P T E M B E R   2

✠

The Martyrs of New Guinea
1942

A reading from the account by Harry Bitmead, a government doctor, of the last words spoken on Sunday, July 26, 1942 by Father Vivian Redlich, Anglican missionary in New Guinea, who was beheaded on a beach near Buna early in August of the same year

After the departure of the boat, Fr Vivian had made his way quickly back to Sangara. He found the Japanese everywhere, and about to destroy the mission.

When I arrived at the shelter there was quite a crowd of natives round about. Fr Vivian spoke to them thus: "I am your missionary. I have come back to you because I knew you would need your father. I am not going to run away from you. I am going to remain to help you as long as you will let me. To-morrow is Sunday. I shall say Mass, and any who wish may communicate." Shortly after dark he returned to the mission house to collect some church equip-

161

ment. He returned about midnight and told me that as yet nothing had been touched in the mission, but the Japanese had told the people of their intention to destroy the place on the Sunday.

Shortly after dawn he woke me up saying: "There is a big number of people here. I am going down to say Mass." He began to vest, and was nearly finished when a native boy rushed to us crying out: "Father! Doctor! Go; do not wait! During the night Embogi came and had a look at where you are, and has just gone to tell the Japanese, because he wants them to come and kill you."

There was a dead silence. I looked at Fr Vivian. He bowed his head in prayer for a few moments, and then said to the people: "To-day is Sunday. It is God's day. I shall say Mass. We shall worship God."

The dense silence of the jungle was broken only by the sound of the priest's voice praying for his people. Then came the rustle of movement as those bare brown feet moved near the altar at the time of Communion.

Brother Kenneth, C.G.A. Saints of the Twentieth Century (revised edition, Oxford, 1987), 138–139; Dorothea Tomkins and Brian Hughes. The Road from Gona (London, 1970), 55–62

SEPTEMBER 9

✠

Constance, Nun, and her Companions
Commonly called "The Martyrs of Memphis," 1878

A reading from the letters of Sister Constance of the Community of St. Mary, one of "The Martyrs of Memphis," written in 1878

A pouring rain—another bad thing—it just stirs up the horrible filth of this wretched city, and leaves muddy pools to stagnate in the sun. There is no drainage—no system of cleaning the city—everyone carries the kitchen refuse into the back alley, and the pigs, which run about the streets, eat it up. I have disinfected this house thoroughly, from garret to cellar, with lime, carbolic acid, and copperas—and today the health officer came and threw tar-water all about the place—spoiling our nice clean galleries and spotting our hall carpeting in the most unnecessary manner.

One comfort we have that we never had before, and perhaps could never have under any other circumstances—the Reservation [of the Blessed Sacrament]—always in the Church. It is not often possible to go in, but we have the key, and it does not take long to run through the little gallery leading from the Community Room. That, and the daily Celebration, do make such a difference in our life here!

Sr. Mary Hilary, C.S.M. Ten Decades of Praise: The Story of the Community of Saint Mary during its First Century (Racine, 1965), 92

SEPTEMBER 12

✠

John Henry Hobart
Bishop of New York, 1830

A reading from A Companion for the Book of Common Prayer *by John Henry Hobart, Bishop of New York, published in 1805*

Forms of prayer possess many important advantages. When public worship is conducted according to a prescribed form, the people are previously acquainted with the prayers in which they are to join, and are thus enabled to render unto GOD a reasonable and enlightened service. In forms of prayer, that dignity and propriety of language, so necessary in supplications addressed to the infinite Majesty of Heaven, may be preserved. They prevent the particular opinions and dispositions of the minister from influencing the devotions of the congregation. They serve as a standard of faith and practice, impressing on both minister and people, at every performance of public worship, the important doctrines and duties of the Gospel. And they render the service more animating by uniting the people with the minister in the performance of public worship.

Thus, then, we see how excellent and superior in all respects is the Liturgy of our Church; and how admirably she has provided for the two important objects of the public service, instruction and devotion. The lessons, the creeds, the commandments, the epistles and gospels contain the most important and impressive instruction on the doctrines and duties of religion. While the confession, the collects, and prayers, the litany and thanksgivings, lead the understanding and the heart through all the sublime and affecting exercises of devotion. In this truly evangelical and excellent Liturgy the Supreme LORD of the universe is invoked by the most appropriate, affecting, and sublime epithets: all the wants to which man, as a dependant and sinful being, is subject are expressed in language at once simple, concise, and comprehensive; these wants are urged by confessions the most humble, and supplications the most reverential and ardent. The all-sufficient merits of JESUS CHRIST, the Savior of the world, are uniformly urged as the only effectual plea, the only certain pledge of divine mercy and grace; and with the most instructive lessons from the sacred oracles and the most profound confessions and supplications is mingled the sublime chorus of praise begun by the minister, and responded with one heart and one voice from the assembled congregation. The mind, continually passing from one exercise of worship to another, and instead of one continued and uniform prayer sending up its wishes and aspirations in short and varied collects and supplications, is never suffered to grow languid or weary.

A person who thus sincerely offers his devotions according to the Liturgy of the Church, may be satisfied that he is worshiping GOD "with the spirit and with the understanding also." The more frequently and seriously he joins in the service, the more will he be impressed with its exquisite beauties, which tend at once to gratify his taste and to quicken his devotion. That continual change of language in prayer which some persons appear to consider as essential to spiritual devotion, it would be impossible to attain, even were every minister left to his own discretion in public worship. The same expressions would necessarily recur frequently in his prayers. They would soon sink into a form destitute of that propriety and dignity of sentiment and language, of that variety, that simplicity, and affecting fervour which characterize the Liturgy of the Church.

Long then may the Church preserve a form of service which is calculated to cherish in her members a spirit of devotion equally remote from dull and unprofitable lukewarmness on the one hand, and from blind, extravagant, and indecent enthusiasm on the other—a form of service which has ever served to brighten the pious graces of her members, and, in the season of declension and error, to preserve the light of divine truth and the genuine spirit of evangelical piety. With such sacred and commendable caution does the Episcopal Church in America guard the Book of Common Prayer that she exacts from all her ministers, at their ordination, a solemn promise of conformity to it; and, in one of her canons, enjoins the use of it "before all sermons and lectures, and on all other occasions of public worship," and forbids the use of any "other prayers than those prescribed in the said book."

A Companion for the Book of Common Prayer (N.Y., edition of 1827), 5, 10–14: Prayer Book Spirituality, ed. J. Robert Wright (N.Y., 1989), 95–100

SEPTEMBER 13

✠

Cyprian

Bishop and Martyr of Carthage, 258

A reading from the treatise On Works and Almsgiving *written c. 253 by Cyprian, Bishop and Martyr of Carthage*

In Scripture the Holy Spirit says: "By works of mercy and by faith sins are purged." [Prov. 16.6] This cannot possibly refer to sins committed before our redemption, for they are purged by the blood of Christ and by sanctification.

Many and great are the blessings which have been and are being ever bestowed on us for our salvation by the boundless mercy of God the Father and Christ. The Father sent the Son to restore us by saving us and giving us life. The Son was content to be sent and to be called Son of Man in order to make us children of God. He humbled himself to exalt a people who were prostrate; he was wounded to heal our wounds; he became a slave to bring to liberty those who were slaves; he underwent death that he might procure immortality for mortals. Such is the measure and the extent of the gifts of the divine love.

But God's providence and God's mercy are not yet fully told. In the plan of our salvation there is provision of still greater care for the preservation of humankind after our redemption. Just as remission of sins is given once for all in baptism, so unremitting and ceaseless service fulfils a role similar to that of baptism by bestowing yet again the mercy of God. The merciful one tells us to do acts of mercy, and, because he wants to preserve those redeemed at so great a cost, he teaches us how we can be cleansed once more if we become defiled after receiving the grace of baptism.

In conclusion, the divine admonition never rests, is never silent. In the Holy Scriptures, both old and new, the people of God at all times and in all places are stirred up to works of mercy. Everyone who is being prepared for the hope of the kingdom of heaven is commanded by the voice and counsel of the Holy Spirit to give alms.

Treatise on Works and Almsgiving 2–4: CSEL 3, 373–376

SEPTEMBER 16

✠

Ninian

Bishop in Galloway, c. 430

A reading from the Ecclesiastical History of England *by Bede the Venerable, Priest and Monk of Jarrow, concerning Ninian, Bishop in Galloway in the early fifth century.*

The southern Picts, who live on this side of the mountains, are said to have abandoned the errors of idolatry long before this date and to have accepted the true faith through the preaching of Bishop Ninian, a most reverend and holy man of British race, who had been regularly instructed in the mysteries of the Christian faith in Rome. Ninian's own episcopal see, named after Saint Martin and famous for its stately church, is now held by the English, and it is here that his body and those of many saints lie at rest. The place belongs to the province of Bernicia and is commonly known as "Candida Casa," or "the White House," because he built the church of stone, which was unusual among the Britons.

Ecclesiastical History 3, 4: Colgrave and Mynors, 222–223

Edward Bouverie Pusey

Priest, 1882

A reading from a Christmas sermon of Edward Bouverie Pusey, Priest, entitled "God With Us"

If we would see [God with us] in his sacraments, we must see him also wherever he has declared himself to be, and especially in his poor. In them also he is "with us" still. And so our church has united mercy to his poor with the sacrament of his Body and Blood, and bade us, ere we approach to receive him, to remember him in his poor, that so, loving much, we, who are otherwise unworthy, may be much forgiven; we, considering him in his poor and needy, may be permitted to behold him; and for him parting with our earthly substance, may be partakers of his heavenly. Real love to Christ must issue in love to all who are Christ's, and real love to Christ's poor must issue in self-denying acts of love towards them. Casual almsgiving is not Christian charity. Rather, seeing Christ in the poor, the sick, the hungry, the thirsty, the naked, we must, if we can, by ourselves, if not by others, seek them out, as we would seek Christ, looking for a blessing from it, far greater than any they can gain from our alms. It was promised of old time, as a blessing, "the poor shall never cease out of the land," and now we know the mercy of this mysterious blessing, for they are the presence of our Lord. "The poor," he saith, "ye have always with you, but me ye have not always," not in bodily presence, but in his poor, whom we shall ever have.

The poor of Christ are the church's special treasure, as the Gospel is their special property, the church the home of the homeless, the mother of the fatherless. The poor are the wealth, the dowry of the church; they have a sacred character about them; they bring a blessing with them; for they are what Christ for our sake made himself. Such as them did he call around him; such as they, whether by God's outward appointment, or by his Spirit directing men's choice, the poor, rich in faith, have been the converters of the world; and we, my brethren, if we are wise, must seek to be like them, to empty ourselves, at least, of our abundance; to empty ourselves, rather, of our self-conceit, our notions of station, our costliness of dress, our jewelry, our luxuries, our self-love, even as he, on this day, emptied himself of the glory which he had with the Father, the brightness of his majesty, the worship of the hosts of heaven, and made himself poor, to make us rich, and to the truly poor he hath promised the kingdom of heaven. The hungry he will fill, but those in themselves rich, he will send empty away. Year by year there is more need; the poor are multiplying upon us, and distress on them; gigantic needs require gigantic efforts; in these our towns, our church is losing its best blessing, that of being the church of the poor; we know not too often of their existence. Our fair houses are like painted sepulchres, hiding, by a goodly outside, from our own sight, the misery, and hunger, and cold, and nakedness, which we love not to look upon, but which will rise in judgment against our nation, if we heed it not.

Realize we that they are Christ's, yea, that we approach to Christ in them, feed him, visit him, clothe him, attend on him, and we shall feel (as saints, even of the noble of this world, have felt) that it is a high honour to us to be admitted to them. Such as can, would gladly devote their lives to them. We all should treat their needs with reverence, not relieving them coldly, and as a form, but humble ourselves in heart before their patient suffering; welcome the intercourse with them, as bringing us nearer unto Christ. In them he comes to us, in them we visit him; in them we may find him; he in them and for them intercedes for us with the Father. In them he who gave them to us, the means and the hearts to relieve them, will

169

receive our gifts. He, before men and angels, shall acknowledge as done to him, what for his sake, we did to them.

E.B. Pusey. Parochial Sermons, vol. 1 (fourth ed., Oxford, 1852), 58–60 (Punctuation and capitalization modernized)

SEPTEMBER 19

✠

Theodore of Tarsus
Archbishop of Canterbury, 690

A reading from the Ecclesiastical History of England *by Bede the Venerable, Priest and Monk of Jarrow, concerning Theodore of Tarsus, Archbishop of Canterbury in the late seventh century*

At this time there was in Rome a monk named Theodore, a native of Tarsus in Cilicia, who was well known to Hadrian. He was learned both in sacred and in secular literature, in Greek and in Latin, of proved integrity, and of the venerable age of sixty-six. Hadrian, therefore, suggested the name of Theodore to the Pope, who agreed to consecrate him, but made it a condition that Hadrian himself should accompany him to Britain, since he had already traveled through Gaul twice on various missions and had both a better knowledge of the road and sufficient companions of his own available. The Pope also ordered Hadrian to give full support to Theodore in his teaching, and to ensure that he did not introduce into the church which he was to rule any Greek customs which conflicted with the teachings of the true faith.

On receiving the subdiaconate, Theodore waited four months

for his hair to grow so that he could receive the circular tonsure; for hitherto he had worn the tonsure of the holy Apostle Paul in conformity to eastern custom. He was then consecrated bishop by Pope Vitalian on Sunday the 26th of March 668, and on the 27th of May he set out for Britain, accompanied by Hadrian.

Theodore arrived in his see and held it for twenty-one years, three months, and twenty-six days. Soon after his arrival, he visited every part of the island occupied by the English peoples, and received a ready welcome and hearing everywhere. He was accompanied and assisted throughout his journey by Hadrian, and he taught the Christian way of life and the canonical method of keeping Easter.

Theodore was the first archbishop whom the entire church of the English obeyed. Both he and Hadrian were men of learning both in sacred and in secular literature. They therefore attracted a large number of students, into whose minds they poured the waters of wholesome knowledge day by day. In addition to instructing them in the Holy Scriptures, they also taught their pupils poetry, astronomy, and the calculation of the church calendar. In proof of this, some of their students still alive today are as proficient in Latin and Greek as in their native tongue. Never had there been such happy times as these since the English settled in Britain. The people eagerly sought the newfound joys of the kingdom of heaven, and all who wished for instruction in the reading of the Scriptures found teachers ready at hand. The knowledge of sacred music, hitherto limited to Kent, now began to spread to all the churches of the English.

Ecclesiastical History 4, 1–2: Colgrave and Mynors, 330–335

✠

John Coleridge Patteson

Bishop of Melanesia, and his Companions, Martyrs, 1871

A reading from an entry in the Journal of John Coleridge Patteson, Bishop of Melanesia, dated in June of 1871, the year of his martyrdom

I *think* that we may, without danger, baptize a great many infants and quite young children—so many parents are actually seeking Christian teaching themselves, or willing to give their children to be taught. I think that some adults, married men, may possibly be baptized. I should think that not less than forty or fifty are daily being taught twice a day, as a distinct set of Catechumens. Besides this, some of the women seem to be in earnest.

About two hours and a half are spent daily by me with about twenty-three grown-up men. They come, too, at all hours, in small parties, two or three, to tell their thoughts and feelings, how they are beginning to pray, what they say, what they wish and hope, etc.

There is more indication than I ever saw here before of a "movement," a distinct advance, towards Christianity. The distinction between passively listening to our teaching, and accepting it as God's Word and acting upon it, seems to be clearly felt. I speak strongly and habitually about the necessity of baptism. "He that believeth, and *is baptized,*" etc. Independently of the doctrinal truth about baptism, the call to the heathen man to take some step, to enter into some engagement, to ally himself with a body of Christian believers by some distinct act of his own, needing careful preparation, etc., has a meaning and a value incalculably great.

Yes, JESUS is to us all a source of pardon, light, and life, all these treasures are in Him. But he distributes these gifts by His Spirit in

His appointed ways. You *can't* understand or receive the Gospel with a heart clinging to your old ways. And you can't remake your hearts. *He* must do it, and this is His way of doing it. You must be born again.

Charlotte Mary Yonge. Life of John Coleridge Patteson, Missionary Bishop of the Melanasian Islands (2 vols., London, 1874), vol. 2, pp. 341–342

SEPTEMBER 25

✠

Sergius

Abbot of Holy Trinity, Moscow, 1392

A reading from the Life of Sergius of Radonezh, *who died in 1392, written by Epiphanius, monk of the Holy Trinity Monastery that Sergius founded*

Prince Mamai had mustered a great army, the entire host of the infidel Tartars, in order to attack the Russian land. And everyone was seized with terror. The ruling prince, who at that time held the scepter of the Russian lands, the praiseworthy and victorious great Dimitri [Donskoi], came to Sergius, for he had great faith in this "staretz." He asked whether Sergius would command him to march against the infidels. The saint gave him his blessing, armed him with prayers, and said: "My Lord, it behooves you to guard the worthy flock entrusted to you by God. You must march against the infidels, and with God's help you shall defeat them and return unhurt to your native land, and you shall merit great praise." The prince [Dimitri] replied: "If God lends me his help, I shall found a monastery in the name of the most pure Mother of God." And having received the saint's blessing, he hastened away. Mustering all his warriors, he marched against the godless Tartars [on the plains of Kulikovo]; but when he saw their powerful host, he held back, and many in his camp were in the grip of fear, not knowing what to do. At that very moment, a messenger appeared, bringing word from the holy man: "My Lord, do not hesitate. March boldly against the fierce enemy. Fear nothing, for God will help you."

Prince Dimitri and his army were inspired with great courage. They attacked the infidels and fought, and many fell, and God helped the great and victorious Dimitri. The Tartars were defeated. At that time the saint, who had the gift of supernatural sight, was praying before God for victory over the pagans. And at the very hour when the infidels were finally routed, Sergius foretold the whole event. He spoke of victory, and of the courage displayed by Prince Dimitri, and he named those who were slain and prayed for their souls to the all-merciful God.

Prince Dimitri returned joyfully to his country and hastened to Sergius. He thanked him for his prayers and for those of his brethren, bestowed a generous gift upon the monastery of the Holy Trinity, and, in fulfillment of his promise, took steps to found a monastery in the name of the most pure Mother of God.

A Treasury of Russian Spirituality, ed. G.P. Fedotov (London, 1952), 77–78

Lancelot Andrewes

Bishop of Winchester, 1626

A reading from the Prayers for Sunday at the beginning of the Private Devotions *of Lancelot Andrewes, Bishop of Winchester, originally composed in Greek and Latin and published posthumously in 1648*

Introduction

Through the tender mercies of our God, the Day-Spring from on high hath visited us.

Commemoration

Glory be to thee, O Lord, glory to thee, Creator of light and Enlightener of the world. Thou who didst create the visible light, the sun's rays, a flame of fire, day and night, evening and morning. Thou who didst create the Light invisible, the Light which never sets, that which may be known of God, the Law written in the heart. Oracle of prophets, melody of psalms, instruction of proverbs, experience of histories, the Light whereof there is no eventide.

Thou who on this day didst rise again, raise up our souls unto newness of life, granting us repentance from dead works, and planting us in the likeness of thy resurrection.

Thou who didst send down on thy disciples on this day thy thrice-holy Spirit, withdraw not thou the gift, O Lord, from us, but renew it in us, day by day, who ask thee for it.

Confession

Merciful and pitiful Lord, long-suffering and of great mercy, I have sinned, Lord, I have sinned against thee.

I conceal nothing, I make not excuses. For me, I forget not my sins, they are ever before me. I remember them in the bitterness of my soul.

I repent, O Lord, I repent. Lord, help thou mine impenitence. And more and still more pierce thou, rend, crush my heart, and remit, forgive, pardon what things are grief to me, and offence of heart.

And in due time, Lord, say to me: Be of good cheer, thy sins are forgiven thee, my grace is sufficient for thee.

Prayer for Grace

Open thou mine eyes that I may see, incline my heart that I may desire, order my steps that I may follow, the way of thy commandments.

Grant me grace to worship thee in spirit and in truth, to reverence thy holy name, to serve thee devoutly and decently, with the gestures of my body, with the praises of my tongue, in private and in public.

Act of Faith

Let my faith in the church entitle me to a part in its calling and election, to sanctification in its holiness, to membership in its universality, to fellowship with the saints, by sharing in their prayers and sacraments, in their watchings and fastings, in their holy sighs and tears, and, if thy providence shall call me to them, in their afflictions and sufferings; by all these establishing me in a firm assurance of thy forgiveness of sins, of the resurrection from death, and of translation to immortal glory.

Intercession

O thou that art the Hope of all the ends of the earth, remember thy whole creation for good, visit the world in thy compassion.

O thou who for this end didst both die and rise, that thou mightest be the Lord both of the dead and living, since whether we live or whether we die still we are thine, O Lord, let thy mercy be ever upon us, both in life and in death.

Commendation

O Lord I commend to thee, my soul and my body, my mind and my thoughts, my prayers and my vows, my senses and my limbs, my words and my works, my life and my death; my brothers and my sisters, and their children, my friends and my benefactors, my well-wishers, my kindred and my neighbours, my country and all Christian people.

Praise

Let us lift up our hearts unto the Lord, as it is meet and right, and fitting and due, in all things and for all things, at all times, in all places, by all means in every season, every spot, ever, everywhere, everyway, to make mention of thee, to worship thee, to give thanks to thee, who art the Maker, Nourisher, Preserver, Governor, Protector, Author, Finisher of all things.

Reverendi Patris Lanceloti Andrews Episcopi Wintoniensis Preces Privatae Quotidianae Graece et Latine, 3rd ed. (London, 1848), 46–85; Florence Higham. Lancelot Andrewes (London, 1952), 114–118

SEPTEMBER 30

✠

Jerome
Priest, and Monk of Bethlehem, 420

A reading from the letter of Jerome to Nepotian, written c. 394

Read the Holy Scriptures constantly. Never, indeed, let the sacred volume be out of your hand. Learn what you have to teach.

"Hold fast the faithful word which is according to the teaching, that you may be able to exhort in sound doctrine and to refute the gainsayers. Continue in the things that you have learned and that have been entrusted to you, knowing of whom you have learned them," and "be always ready to give an answer to every person who asks you a reason for the hope that is within you." Do not let your deeds belie your words, lest when you speak in church someone may mentally reply: "Why do you not practice what you preach?" It is self-contradiction for a master, with stomach full, to read a homily on fasting! A robber might just as well accuse others of covetousness! In a priest of Christ mind and mouth should be in harmony.

When teaching in church, try to evoke not applause but lamentation. Let the tears of your hearers be your glory. A presbyter's words ought to be seasoned by the reading of Scripture. Be not a declaimer or a ranter, one who gabbles without rhyme or reason, but show yourself skilled in the deep things and versed in the mysteries of God. To roll your words out and by your quickness of utterance to astonish the unlettered crowd is a mark of ignorance. Assurance often explains that of which it knows nothing, and when it has convinced others it claims knowledge for itself. There is nothing so easy as by sheer volubility to deceive a common crowd or an uneducated congregation. Such a group most admires that which they fail to understand.

Many people build the walls of churches nowadays, but without pillars to support them. Their marbles gleam, their ceilings glitter with gold, their altars are studded with jewels; yet to the choice of Christ's ministers no heed is paid. And let no one object against me the wealth of the temple in Judea, its altar, its lamps, its censers, its dishes, its cups, its spoons, and the rest of its golden vessels. If these were approved by the Lord it was at a time when the priests had to offer victims and when the blood of sheep was the redemption of sins. They were figures typifying things still future and were "written for our admonition upon whom the ends of the world are come." But now our Lord by his poverty has consecrated the poverty of his house. Let us, therefore, think of his cross and count riches to be but dirt.

Letter 52, 7–8, 10: Loeb 206–217

OCTOBER 1

✠

Remigius
Bishop of Rheims, c. 530

A reading from the History of the Franks *by Gregory of Tours, historian, concerning the conversion of Clovis, King of the Franks, by Remigius, Bishop of Rheims, who died c. 530*

Then the queen commanded the holy Remigius, bishop of Rheims, to be summoned secretly, entreating him to impart the word of salvation to the king. The bishop, calling the king to him in private, began to instil into him faith in the true God, maker of heaven and earth, and urged him to forsake his idols, which were unable to help either himself or others. But Clovis replied: "I myself, most holy father, will gladly hearken to you; but one thing yet remains. The people that follow me will not allow that I forsake their gods; yet I will go, and reason with them according to your word." But when he came before the assembled people, all the people cried with one voice: "O gracious king, we drive forth our gods that perish and we are ready to follow the God who perishes not, the God preached by Remigius."

News of this was brought to the bishop, who was filled with great joy and commanded the font to the prepared. The streets were overshadowed with colored hangings, the churches adorned with white hangings, the baptistery was set in order, smoke of incense spread in clouds, perfumed tapers gleamed, the whole church about the place of baptism was filled with divine fragrance. And now the king first demanded to be baptized by the bishop. Like a new Constantine he moved forward to the water, to blot out the former leprosy, to wash away in this new stream the foul stains borne from old days. As he entered to be baptized, the saint of God spoke these words with eloquent lips: "Meekly bow your proud head, Sicamber; adore that which you have burned, burn that which you have adored." For the holy Remigius, the bishop, was of excellent learning, and above all skilled in the art of rhetoric, and so exemplary in holiness.

The king therefore, confessing Almighty God, three in one, was baptized in the name of the Father, the Son, and the Holy Ghost, and anointed with holy chrism, with the sign of the cross of Christ. Of his army were baptized more than three thousand; and his sister Albofled, who not long after was taken to the Lord, was likewise baptized.

History of the Franks 2, 31: transl. O.M. Dalton (2 vols., Oxford, 1927), vol. 2, 65–70

✠

Francis of Assisi
Friar, 1226

A *reading from the* Franciscan Rule of 1223

I counsel, warn, and exhort my brothers in the Lord Jesus Christ that when they go out into the world they shall not be quarrelsome or contentious, nor judge others. But they shall be gentle, peaceable, and kind, mild and humble, and virtuous in speech, as is becoming to all. They shall not ride on horseback unless compelled by manifest necessity or infirmity to do so. When they enter a house they shall say: "Peace be to this house." According to the holy Gospel, they may eat of whatever food is set before them.

I strictly forbid all the brothers to accept money or property either in person or through another. Nevertheless, for the needs of the sick, and for clothing the other brothers, the ministers and guardians may, as they see that necessity requires, provide through spiritual friends, according to the locality, season, and the degree of cold which may be expected in the region where they live. But, as has been said, they shall never receive money or property.

Those brothers to whom the Lord has given the ability to work shall work faithfully and devotedly, so that idleness, which is the enemy of the soul, may be excluded and not extinguish the spirit of prayer and devotion to which all temporal things should be subservient. As the price of their labors they may receive things that are necessary for themselves and the brothers, but not money or property. And they shall humbly receive what is given them, as is becoming to the servants of God and to those who practice the most holy poverty.

The brothers shall have nothing of their own, neither house, nor land, nor anything, but as pilgrims and strangers in this world, serving the Lord in poverty and humility, let them confidently go asking alms. Nor let them be ashamed of this, for the Lord made himself poor for us in this world. This is the highest degree of poverty which has made you, my dearest brothers, heirs and kings of the kingdom of heaven, which has made you poor in goods, and exalted you in virtues. Let this be your portion, which leads into the land of the living. Cling wholly to this, my most beloved brothers, and you shall wish to have in this world nothing else than the name of the Lord Jesus Christ.

Franciscan Rule of 1223, 3–6: Omnibus, ed. Habig (Chicago, 1983), 60–61

OCTOBER 6

✠

William Tyndale
Priest, 1536

A reading from the Prologue upon the Epistle to the Romans *published by William Tyndale, Priest and Bible translator, in 1526*

Herewith St Paul [in the fourth chapter of his Epistle to the Romans] now establisheth his doctrine of faith, rehearsed afore in chapter three, and bringeth also the testimony of David, Psalm thirty-two, which calleth a man blessed, not of works, but in that his sin is not reckoned, and in that faith is imputed for righteousness, although he abide not afterward without good works, when he is once justified. For we are justified, and receive the Spirit, for to do good works; neither were it otherwise possible to do good works, except we first had the Spirit.

October 6

For how is it possible to do any thing well in the sight of God, while we are yet in captivity and bondage under the devil, and the devil possesseth us altogether, and holdeth our hearts, so that we cannot once consent unto the will of God? No man therefore can [go before] the Spirit in doing good. The Spirit must first come, and wake him out of his sleep with the thunder of the law, and fear him, and shew him his miserable estate and wretchedness; and make him abhor and hate himself, and to desire help; and then comfort him again with the pleasant rain of the gospel, that is to say, with the sweet promises of God in Christ, and stir up faith in him to believe the promises. Then, when he believeth the promises, as God was merciful to promise, so is he true to fulfil them, and will give him the Spirit and strength, both to love the will of God, and to work thereafter. So we see that God only, who, according to the scripture, worketh all in all things, worketh a man's justifying, salvation, and health; yea, and poureth faith and belief, lust to love God's will, and strength to fulfil the same, into us, even as water is poured into a vessel; and that of his good will and purpose, and not of our deservings and merits. God's mercy in promising, and truth in fulfilling his promises, saveth us, and not we ourselves; and therefore is all laud, praise, and glory to be given unto God for his mercy and truth, and not unto us for our merits and deservings.

Doctrinal Treatises and Introductions to Different Portions of the Holy Scriptures by William Tyndale, ed. Henry Walter (Parker Society, Cambridge, 1848), 497–498

✠

Robert Grosseteste

Bishop of Lincoln, 1253

A reading from a letter to Pope Innocent IV and the Cardinals written in 1250 by Robert Grosseteste, Bishop of Lincoln

What is the first cause and origin of these great evils? I fear to speak it, but yet I dare not be silent, lest I should merit the reproach of the prophet: "Woe is me, because I have held my peace!" The cause, the fountain, the origin of all this, is the court of Rome, not only because it does not put to flight these evils and purge away these abominations when it alone has the power to do so and is pledged most fully in that sense; but still more because by its dispensations, provisions, and collations to the pastoral care, it appoints in the full light of the sun persons such as I have described, not pastors but destroyers. Moreover, so that it may provide for the livelihood of some one person, it hands over to the jaws of death many thousands of souls, for the life of each one of which the Son of God was willing to be condemned to a most shameful death. Whoever does not hinder this when able, is involved in the same crime; and the crime is greater in proportion as the one who commits it is more highly placed, and the cause of evil is worse than its effect.

Nor let any one say that this court acts thus for the common advantage of the church. This common advantage was studied by the holy fathers who endured suffering on this account; it can never be advanced by that which is unlawful or evil. Woe to those who say: "Let us do evil that good may come!" Pastoral cure does not consist alone in administering the sacraments, repeating the canonical hours, and celebrating masses—and even these offices are seldom performed by mercenaries—but in the teaching of the living truth, the condemnation of vice, the punishment of it when necessary, and this but rarely can the mercenaries dare to do. It consists also in feeding the hungry, giving drink to the thirsty, clothing the naked, receiving guests, and visiting the sick and those in prison, especially those who belong to the parish and have a claim on the endowment of the church. These duties cannot be performed by deputies or hirelings, especially as they hardly receive out of the goods of the church enough to support their own lives. This bad use of church office is greatly to be lamented in the case of the non-monastic clergy, but in their case, at any rate, there is always the possibility that others of a better mind may follow them. When, however, parish churches are appropriated to religious houses, these evils are made permanent.

Those who preside in the see of Rome are in a special degree the representatives of Christ, and in that character are bound to exhibit the works of Christ, and to that extent are entitled to be obeyed in all things. If, however, through favoritism or on other grounds they command what is opposed to the precepts and will of Christ, they separate themselves from Christ and from the conception of what a Pope should be. Then they are guilty of apostasy themselves and become a cause of apostasy in others. God forbid that such should be the case in this see! Let its occupants, therefore, take heed lest they do or enjoin anything which is at variance with the will of Christ.

F.S. Stevenson. Robert Grosseteste (London, 1899), 286–288

OCTOBER 14

✠

Samuel Isaac Joseph Schereschewsky
Bishop of Shanghai, 1906

A reading from An Appeal for Establishing a Missionary College in China *written by Samuel Isaac Joseph Schereschewsky, Bishop of Shanghai, in 1877*

From the earliest days of the Church, education has been an important agent in the propagation of Christianity. During the middle ages education was one of the chief instrumentalities by which Christianity was introduced among European nations. Rome has always availed herself of this power, both to extend her dominion and to regain lost ground. And if education has been an element of such importance in establishing Christianity in the West, have we any reason to believe that it will be a less powerful agent in establishing Christianity in the East? Not only so, but it seems to me that our endeavor to propagate the Christian religion *among* such a people as the Chinese (without it), would be most unwise, for among heathen nations there are few where literature is so identified with the national life. It is only necessary as a proof of this to refer to the vastness of their literature, and the profound respect that is accorded to the pursuit of learning and literary men. A "literary degree" is the "open sesame" to all avenues of distinction in China, and in that land above all others the influence of such an institution as the one proposed could hardly fail to produce results exceeding perhaps our most sanguine expectations.

Again, the better one is acquainted with the state of things in China, and the more one studies the Chinese people with an heartfelt desire for their speedy conversion to Christianity, the more strongly one is convinced that the most effective agency that can be employed in carrying on the great work of evangelizing that nation, must be thoroughly-trained native ministers, who shall go forth to proclaim the Gospel with a might and power which only a native ministry can possess.

And from another writing by Bishop Schereschewsky:

There have, indeed, been missionaries who, almost immediately after their arrival, having picked up a few broken phrases, commenced, as they supposed, to preach the Gospel to the heathen, but which preaching most likely consisted in nothing more than uttering some sounds wholly unintelligible to the hearers. It can fairly be asserted that preaching the Gospel in such a manner is exhibiting a zeal without much knowledge. The Gospel of Christ is to be made honorable in every respect. Now, to preach in an incomprehensible gibberish to such a people as the Chinese, who, perhaps, more than any other people, are fastidious about language, is anything but making it honorable.

In my humble opinion it will require at least eighteen months' very hard study before one would be enabled to express himself on any topic, not belonging to the routine of common life, intelligibly and clearly in a foreign tongue. This is true with reference to all other languages—some of the easy European languages, perhaps, excepted—but more especially is this the case with regard to the Chinese language. I say Chinese *language;* I should rather say the Chinese *languages,* for really one desiring to become usefully familiar with the speech of China has to study at least two, if not three distinct languages.

An Appeal for Establishing a Missionary College in China (Philadelphia, 17 March 1877); James Arthur Muller. Apostle of China: Samuel Isaac Joseph Schereschewsky 1831–1906 (N.Y., 1937), 44

Teresa of Avila

Nun, 1582

A reading from a work by Teresa of Avila, Spanish Carmelite Nun and Mystic of the sixteenth century

If Christ Jesus dwells in one of us as friend and noble leader, that person can endure all things, for Christ helps and strengthens us and never abandons us. He is a true friend. And I clearly see that if we expect to please him and receive an abundance of his graces, God desires that these graces must come to us from the hands of Christ, through his most sacred humanity, in which God takes delight.

Many, many times I have perceived this through experience. The Lord has told it to me. I have definitely seen that we must enter by this gate if we wish his Sovereign Majesty to reveal to us great and hidden mysteries. We should desire no other path, even if we are at the summit of contemplation; on this road we walk safely. All blessings come to us through our Lord. He will teach us, for in beholding his life we find that he is the best example.

What more do we desire from such a good friend at our side? Unlike our friends in the world, the Lord will never abandon us when we are troubled or distressed. Blessed is the one who truly loves him and always keeps him near. Let us consider the glorious Saint Paul: it seems that no other name fell from his lips than that of Jesus, because the name of Jesus was fixed and embedded in his heart. Once I had come to understand this truth, I carefully considered the lives of some of the saints, the great contemplatives, and found that they took no other path: Francis, Anthony of Padua, Bernard, Catherine of Siena. A person must walk along this path in freedom, placing oneself in God's hands. If God should desire to raise us to the position of one who is an intimate and shares his secrets, we ought to accept this gladly.

Whenever we think of Christ we should recall the love that led him to bestow on us so many graces and favors, and also the great love God showed in giving us in Christ a pledge of his love; for love calls for love in return. Let us strive to keep this always before our eyes and to rouse ourselves to love him. For if at some time the Lord should grant us the grace of impressing his love on our hearts, all will become easy for us and we shall accomplish great things quickly and without effort.

Opusculum De libro vitae 22, 6–7, 14

OCTOBER 16

✠

Hugh Latimer and Nicholas Ridley
Bishops, 1555

Thomas Cranmer
Archbishop of Canterbury, 1556

A reading from the Sermon of the Plough *by Hugh Latimer, Bishop of Worcester and reformer, preached at Paul's Cross in London on January 18, 1548*

I told you in my first sermon, honourable audience, that I purposed to declare unto you two things. The one, what seed should be sown in God's field, in God's plough land; and the other, who

189

should be the sowers: that is to say, what doctrine is to be taught in Christ's church and congregation, and what men should be the teachers and preachers of it. The first part I have told you in the three sermons past, in which I have assayed to set forth my plough, to prove what I could do. And now I shall tell you who be the ploughers: for God's word is a seed to be sown in God's field, that is, the faithful congregation, and the preacher is the sower. And it is in the gospel: "He that soweth, the husbandman, the plough-man, went forth to sow his seed." So that a preacher is resembled to a ploughman, as it is in another place: "No man that putteth his hand to the plough, and looketh back, is apt for the kingdom of God." That is to say, let no preacher be negligent in doing his office. For preaching of the gospel is one of God's plough-works, and the preacher is one of God's ploughmen.

I liken preaching to a ploughman's labour, and a prelate to a ploughman. But now you will ask me, whom I call a prelate? A prelate is that man, whatsoever he be, that hath a flock to be taught of him; whosoever hath any spiritual charge in the faithful congregation, and whosoever he be that hath cure of souls. And well may the preacher and the ploughman be likened together: first, for their labour of all seasons of the year; for there is no time of the year in which the ploughman hath not some special work to do. And then they also may be likened together for the diversity of works and variety of offices that they have to do. For as the plough-man first setteth forth his plough, and then tilleth his land, and breaketh it in furrows, and sometime ridgeth it up again; and at another time harroweth it and clotteth it, and sometime dungeth it and hedgeth it, diggeth it and weedeth it, purgeth and maketh it clean: so the prelate, the preacher, hath many diverse offices to do. He hath first a busy work to bring his parishioners to a right faith, as Paul calleth it, and not a swerving faith; but to a faith that embraceth Christ, and trusteth to his merits; a lively faith, a justify-ing faith; a faith that maketh a man righteous, without respect of works: as ye have it very well declared and set forth in the Homily.

He hath then a busy work, I say, to bring his flock to a right faith, and then to confirm them in the same faith: now casting them down with the law, and with threatenings of God for sin; now ridging them up again with the gospel, and with the promises of God's favour: now weeding them, by telling them their faults, and making them forsake sin; now clotting them, by breaking their stony hearts, and by making them supplehearted, and making them to have hearts of flesh; that is, soft hearts, and apt for doctrine to enter in: now teaching to know God rightly, and to know their duty to God and their neighbours: now exhorting them, when they know their duty, that they do it, and be diligent in it; so that they have a continual work to do.

By this, then, it appeareth that a prelate, or any that hath cure of soul, must diligently and substantially work and labour. Therefore saith Paul to Timothy: "He that desireth to have the office of a bishop, or a prelate, that man desireth a good work." Then if it be a good work, it is work; ye can make but a work of it. It is God's work, God's plough, and that plough God would have still going. Such then as loiter and live idly, are not good prelates, or ministers. And of such as do not preach and teach, nor do their duties, God saith by his prophet Jeremy: "Cursed be the man that doth the work of God fraudulently, guilefully or deceitfully"; some books have it "negligently or slackly." How many such prelates, how many such bishops, Lord, for thy mercy, are there now in England! And what shall we in this case do? shall we company with them? O Lord, for thy mercy! shall we not company with them? O Lord, whither shall we flee from them? But "cursed be he that doth the work of God negligently or guilefully." A sore word for them that are negligent in discharging their office, or have done it fraudulently; for that is the thing that maketh the people ill.

And now I would ask a strange question: who is the most diligentest bishop and prelate in all England, that passeth all the rest in doing his office? I can tell, for I know him who it is; I know him well. But now I think I see you listening and hearkening that I should name him. There is one that passeth all the other, and is the most diligent prelate and preacher in all England. And will ye know who it is? I will tell you: it is the devil. He is the most diligent preacher of all other; he is never out of his diocese; he is never from his cure; ye shall never find him unoccupied; he is ever in his parish; he keepeth residence at all times; ye shall never find him out of the way, call for him when you will he is ever at home; the diligentest preacher in all the realm; he is ever at his plough.

Sermons by Hugh Latimer, Sometime Bishop of Worcester, ed. George E. Corrie (Parker Society, Cambridge, 1844), 59–70

O C T O B E R   1 7

✠

Ignatius
Bishop of Antioch, and Martyr, c. 115

A reading from the Letter to the Smyrnaeans *by Ignatius, Bishop of Antioch and Martyr of the early second century*

Those who have wrong notions about the grace of Jesus Christ, which has come to us, are at variance with God's mind. They care nothing about love: they have no concern for widows or orphans, for the oppressed, for those in prison or released, for the hungry or the thirsty. They hold aloof from the Eucharist and from services of prayer, because they refuse to admit that the Eucharist is the flesh of our Savior Jesus Christ, which suffered for our sins and which, in his goodness, the Father raised [from the dead]. Consequently those who wrangle and dispute God's gift face death. They would have done better to love and so share in the resurrection. The right thing to do, then, is to avoid such people and to talk about them neither in private nor in public. Rather pay attention to the prophets and above all to the Gospel. There we get a clear picture of the Lord's passion and see that the resurrection has really happened.

Flee from schism as the source of evil. You should all follow the bishop as Jesus Christ did the Father. Follow, too, the presbytery as you would the apostles, and respect the deacons as you would God's command. Nobody must do anything that has to do with the church without the bishop's approval. You should regard that Eucharist as valid which is celebrated either by the bishop or by someone the bishop authorizes. Where the bishop is present, there let the congregation gather, just as where Jesus Christ is, there is the Catholic Church.

To the Smyrnaeans 6,2–8,2: Loeb 1, 258–261

OCTOBER 19

✠

Henry Martyn
Priest, and Missionary to India and Persia, 1812

A reading from three letters of Henry Martyn, Priest, and Missionary to India and Persia, written in 1811 and 1812

[*October 1811*] My translator comes about sunrise, corrects a little, and is off, and I see no more of him for the day. Meanwhile I sit fretting, or should do so, as I did at first, were it not for a blessed employment, which so beguiles the tediousness of the day, that I hardly perceive it passing. It is the study of the Psalms in the Hebrew. I have long had it in contemplation, in the assurance, from the number of flat and obscure passages that occur in the translations, that the original has not been hitherto perfectly understood.

Persia is, in many respects, a field ripe for the harvest. Vast numbers secretly hate and despise the superstition imposed on them, and as many of them as have heard the gospel approve it; but they dare not hazard their lives for the name of the Lord Jesus.

Though I have complained above of the inactivity of my translator, I have reason to bless the Lord that he thus supplies Gibeonites for the help of his true Israel. They are employed in a work, of the importance of which they are unconscious, and are making provision for future Persian saints, whose time is, I suppose, now near. Roll back, ye crowded years, your thick array! Let the long, long period of darkness and sin at last give way to the brighter hours of light and liberty, which wait on the wings of the sun of righteousness. Perhaps we witness the dawn of the day of glory; and if not, the desire that we feel, that Jesus may be glorified, and the nations acknowledge his sway, is the earnest of the Spirit, that when he shall appear, we shall also appear with him in glory.

[*January 1812*] Spared by mercy to see the beginning of another year. The last has been in some respects a memorable year; transported in safety to Shiraz, I have been led by the particular providence of God to undertake a work, the idea of which never entered my mind till my arrival here, but which has gone on without material interruption, and is now nearly finished. To all appearance, the present year will be more perilous than any I have seen; but if I live to complete the Persian New Testament, my life after that will be of less importance. But whether life or death be mine, may Christ be magnified in me! If he has work for me to do, I cannot die.

[*July 1812*] We who are in Jesus have the privilege of viewing life and death as nearly the same, since both are one; and I thank a gracious Lord, that sickness never came at a time when I was more free from apparent reasons for living. Nothing seemingly remains for me to do, but to follow the rest of my family to the tomb. Let not the book written against Mahommedanism be published, till approved in India. A European, who has not lived amongst them, cannot imagine how differently they see, imagine, reason, object, from what we do. This I had full opportunity of observing during my eleven months residence at Shiraz. During that time I was engaged in a written controversy with one of the most learned and temperate doctors there. He began. I replied what was unanswerable; then I subjoined a second more direct attack on the glaring absurdities of Mahommedanism, with a statement of the nature and evidences of Christianity. The Soofies then as well as himself desired a demonstration from the very beginning, of the truth of any revelation. As this third treatise contained an examination of the doctrine of the Soofies, and pointed out that their object was attainable by the Gospel, and by that only, it was read with interest, and convinced many. There is not a single Europeanism in the whole that I know of, as my friend and interpreter would not write anything that he could not perfectly comprehend. But I am exhausted; pray for me.

Journal and Letters of the Rev. Henry Martyn, B.D., ed. S. Wilberforce (N.Y., 1851), 455, 456, 460, 463

✠

Alfred the Great
King of the West Saxons, 899

A reading from the Life of Alfred the Great, *King of the West Saxons in the later ninth century, written by Asser, monk and chronicler*

Meanwhile the king, in the midst of wars and frequent hindrances of this present life, and also of the raids of the pagans and his daily infirmities of body, did not cease, single-handed, assiduously and eagerly with all his might, to govern the kingdom, to practice every branch of hunting, to instruct his goldsmiths and all his craftsmen, and his falconers, hawkers and dog-keepers, to erect buildings to his own new design more stately and magnificent than had been the custom of his ancestors, to recite Saxon books, and especially to learn by heart Saxon poems, and command others to do so. He also was in the habit of hearing daily the divine office, the Mass, and certain prayers and psalms, and of observing both the day and the night hours, and of visiting churches at night-time, as we have said, in order to pray without his followers knowing. Moreover, he showed zeal for almsgiving, and generosity both to those of his own country and to strangers from all nations, and very great and matchless kindness and pleasantness toward all people, and skill in searching into things unknown.

Many persons: Franks, Frisians, people of Gaul, pagans, Welsh, Scots and Bretons, willingly submitted to his lordship, both nobles and persons of humble rank. He ruled them all in accordance with his own honorable nature just like his own people, and loved and honored them, and enriched them with money and rights. He was accustomed to listen to the Holy Scripture recited by native clergy, but also, if by chance someone had come from elsewhere, to listen with equal earnestness and attention to prayers along with foreigners. He also loved his bishops and all the ecclesiastical order, his ealdormen and his nobles, his officials and all members of his household, with a wonderful affection. And he himself never ceased among other occupations, day and night, to train their youth, who were being brought up in the royal household, in all good behavior, and to educate them in letters, loving them no less than his own offspring.

Life of King Alfred 76: English Historical Documents 1, ed. Dorothy Whitelock (London, 1968), 267–268

OCTOBER 29

✠

James Hannington

Bishop of Eastern Equatorial Africa, and his Companions, Martyrs, 1885

A reading from the last two days of the diary of James Hannington, Bishop of Eastern Equatorial Africa, written in the year 1885 when he and his Companions were martyred

Wednesday, October 28th.—(Seventh day's prison.) A terrible night, first with noisy, drunken guard, and secondly with vermin, which have found out my tent and swarm. I don't think I got one hour's sound sleep, and woke with fever fast developing. O Lord, do have mercy upon me and release me. I am quite broken down and brought low. Comforted by reading Psalm xxvii.

October 29

In an hour or two fever developed rapidly. My tent was so stuffy that I was obliged to go inside the filthy hut, and soon was delirious.

Evening: fever passed away. Word came that Mwanga had sent three soldiers, but what news they bring they will not yet let me know.

Much comforted by Psalm xxviii.

Thursday, October 29th.—(Eighth day's prison.) I can hear no news, but was held up by Psalm xxx., which came with great power. A hyena howled near me last night, smelling a sick man, but I hope it is not to have me yet.

E.C. Dawson, editor of the Diary, comments:

These are the last words in the little pocket-diary. The ink was perhaps scarcely dry when the Bishop was led forth to his death. The following extract from a recent letter of his able and devoted successor, Bishop Parker, who so manfully stepped into the breach, and who, like the First Bishop, has been so swiftly struck down on the shore of the fatal Lake, throws further light upon the manner in which he faced and met "the last Enemy":—

Ukutu, who was with the Bishop constantly during his imprisonment, and undid his hands when they bound him to lead him off to the spot where he was murdered, told us that as the Bishop walked to that spot he was singing hymns nearly all the way. As they were in English, he did not know their meaning; but he noticed that in them the word JESUS came very frequently.

The Last Journals of Bishop Hannington, ed. E.C. Dawson (London, 1888), 237–239

NOVEMBER 2

✠

All Faithful Departed

A reading from the Treatise on Death *by Cyprian, Bishop and Martyr of Carthage, written on the outbreak of a plague in the year 252*

We should not mourn for our fellow humans who have been freed from this world by the summons of the Lord, since we know that they are not lost but have been sent before us. In departing, they lead the way. As travelers, as voyagers, they should be longed for, but not lamented. Neither should dark clothing be worn here, inasmuch as they have already assumed white garments there.

Let us give the pagans no occasion to censure us deservedly and justly, on the ground that we grieve for those, as if entirely destroyed and lost, who we say are living with God. Let them not censure us on the ground that we do not show by the testimony of the heart and breast the faith which we declare in speech and word! We are prevaricators of our hope and faith, if what we say seems pretended, feigned, and falsified. It is of no value to show forth virtue in words but destroy truth in deeds.

Furthermore, the apostle Paul rebukes and blames any who may be sorrowful at the death of their dear ones: "We would have you be clear," he says, "about those who sleep in death; otherwise you might yield to grief, like those who have no hope. For if we believe that Jesus died and rose, God will bring forth with him from the dead those also who have fallen asleep believing in him."

Our Lord Jesus Christ himself admonishes us, saying: "I am the resurrection and the life: those who believe in me, even though they die, will live; and everyone who lives and believes in me will never die." If we believe in Christ let us have faith in his words and promises, that we who are not to die forever may come in joyful certainty to Christ with whom we are to conquer and reign for eternity.

As to the fact that meanwhile we die, we pass by death to immortality. Eternal life can not succeed unless it has befallen us to depart from the here and now. This is not an end but a passage, a crossing over to eternity. Who would not hasten to better things? Who would not pray to be more quickly changed and reformed to the image of Christ and to the dignity of heavenly grace, since the apostle Paul declares: "We have our citizenship in heaven; it is from there that we eagerly await the coming of our Savior, the Lord Jesus Christ. He will give a new form to this lowly body of ours and remake it according to the pattern of his glorified body."

Let us embrace the day which assigns each of us to an [eternal] dwelling, which on our being rescued from this life and released from the snares of the world, restores us to paradise and the kingdom. What person, after being abroad, would not hasten to return to one's own country? Who, when hurrying to sail to one's family, would not more eagerly long for a favorable wind so that one might more quickly embrace those who are loved?

We account paradise our own country. A great number of our dear ones there await us, parents, sisters and brothers, children. A dense and copious throng longs for us, already secure in their safety but still anxious for our salvation. To these, my beloved, let us hasten with eager longing! Let us pray that it may befall us speedily to be with them, speedily to come to Christ.

Treatise on Death 20–22, 26: PL 4, 596–597, 601–602

✠

Richard Hooker
Priest, 1600

A reading from the Preface and from Book V of the Laws of
Ecclesiastical Polity *by Richard Hooker, Priest, and chief apologist for Anglicanism under Queen Elizabeth I*

Though for no other cause, yet for this; that posterity may know we have not loosely through silence permitted things to pass away as in a dream, there shall be for men's information extant thus much concerning the present state of the Church of God established amongst us, and their careful endeavour which would have upheld the same.

[From Book V:]

Between the throne of God in heaven and his Church upon earth here militant if it be so that Angels have their continual intercourse, where should we find the same more verified than in these two ghostly exercises, the one Doctrine, and the other Prayer? For what is the assembling of the Church to learn, but the receiving of Angels descended from above? What to pray, but the sending of Angels upward? His heavenly inspirations and our holy desires are as so many Angels of intercourse and commerce between God and us. As teaching bringeth us to know that God is our supreme truth; so prayer testifieth that we acknowledge him our sovereign good.

This holy and religious duty of service towards God concerneth us one way in that we are men, and another way in that we are joined as parts to that visible mystical body which is his Church. As men, we are at our own choice, both for time, and place, and form, according to the exigence of our own occasions in private; but the service, which we do as members of a public body, is public, and for that cause must needs be accounted by so much worthier than the other, as a whole society of such condition exceedeth the worth of any one.

When we publicly make our prayers, it cannot be but that we do it with much more comfort than in private, for that the things we ask publicly are approved as needful and good in the judgment of all, we hear them sought for and desired with common consent. Again, thus much help and furtherance is more yielded, in that if so be our zeal and devotion to Godward be slack, the alacrity and fervour of others serveth as a present spur. Finally, the good which we do by public prayer is more than in private can be done, for that besides the benefit which here is no less procured to ourselves, the whole Church is much bettered by our good example; and consequently whereas secret neglect of our duty in this kind is but only our own hurt, one man's contempt of the common prayer of the Church of God may be and oftentimes is most hurtful unto many.

Affirming that the house of prayer is a Court beautified with the presence of celestial powers; that there we stand, we pray, we sound forth hymns unto God, having his Angels intermingled as our associates; and that with reference hereunto the Apostle doth require so great care to be had of decency for the Angels' sake; how can we come to the house of prayer, and not be moved with the very glory of the place itself, so to frame our affections praying, as doth best beseem them, whose suits the Almighty doth there sit to hear, and his Angels attend to further?

Of the Laws of Ecclesiastical Polity, Preface (1594) and Book V (1597); edit. Everyman's Library (New York, 1907/1965), vol. 1, 77–78; vol. 2, 105, 107–109; Prayer Book Spirituality, ed. J. Robert Wright (N.Y., 1989), 23–25

Willibrord

Archbishop of Utrecht, Missionary to Frisia, 739

A reading from Alcuin's Life of Willibrord, *Archbishop of Utrecht and Missionary to Frisia, who died at Echternach on 7 November 739*

[Willibrord said to the King of Fositeland:] "The object of your worship, O King, is not a god but a devil, and he holds you ensnared in rank falsehood in order that he may deliver your soul to eternal fire. For there is no God but one, who created heaven and earth, the seas and all that is in them; and those who worship him in true faith will possess eternal life. As His servant I call upon you this day to renounce the empty and inveterate errors to which your forebears have given their assent and to believe in the one almighty God, our Lord Jesus Christ. Be baptized in the fountain of life and wash away all your sins, so that, forsaking all wickedness and unrighteousness, you may henceforth live as a new man in temperance, justice and holiness. If you do this you will enjoy everlasting glory with God and his saints; but if you spurn me, who set before you the way of life, be assured that with the devil whom you obey you will suffer unending punishment and the flames of hell." At this the King was astonished and replied: "It is clear to me that my threats leave you unmoved and that your words are as uncompromising as your deeds." But although he would not believe the preaching of the truth, he sent back Willibrord with all honour to Pippin, King of the Franks.

Pippin was delighted at his return and begged him to persevere in his divinely appointed task of preaching the Word of God and to root out idolatrous practices and sow the good seed in one place after another. This the devoted preacher strove to carry out with characteristic energy. He traversed every part of the country, exhorting the people in cities, villages and forts where he had previously preached the Gospel to remain loyal to the faith and to their good resolutions. And as the number of the faithful increased day by day and a considerable multitude of believers came to the knowledge of God's Word, many began in their zeal for the faith to make over to the man of God their hereditary properties. These he accepted. Shortly afterwards he ordered churches to be built there, and he appointed priests and deacons to serve them, so that the new converts should have places where they could assemble on feast days and listen to wholesome instruction and where they could learn the principles of the Christian religion from those servants of God who had baptized them. Thus the man of God, favoured by divine grace, made increasing progress from day to day.

It came about, however, that Pippin, King of the Franks, died, and his son Charles became head of the realm. Charles brought many nations under the power of the Franks. At that time Willibrord was officially appointed to preach to the Frisian people, and his episcopal see was fixed at the fortress of Utrecht.

The Anglo-Saxon Missionaries in Germany, transl. and ed. C.H. Talbot (N.Y., 1954), 10–12

✠

Leo the Great

Bishop of Rome, 461

A reading from the "Tome" of Leo the Great, Bishop of Rome, written in 449

As the Word does not withdraw from equality with the Father in glory, so the flesh does not surrender the nature of humankind. For, as we must often say, he is truly Son of God and truly Son of Man: God, inasmuch as "In the beginning was the Word, and the Word was with God, and the Word was God"; and human, inasmuch as "The Word was made flesh and dwelt among us." He is God, inasmuch as "All things were made by him and without him nothing was made"; and human, inasmuch as he was "made of a woman, made under the law." The nativity of the flesh is a manifestation of human nature; the Virgin's child-bearing is an indication of divine power. The infancy of the child is shown by the lowliness of his cradle; the greatness of the Most High is declared by the voices of angels. He whom Herod impiously tries to slay is like humanity in its beginnings, but he whom the Magi are glad humbly to adore is Lord of all.

Even as early as the time when he came to the baptism of John his forerunner, lest the fact that the Godhead was hidden by the veil of flesh should escape notice, the voice of the Father spoke in thunder from heaven: "This is my beloved Son, in whom I am well pleased." Accordingly, he who as man is tempted by the devil's subtlety is the same to whom, as God, angels render duteous service. To hunger, to thirst, to be weary, and to sleep is evidently human; but to feed five thousand with five loaves, and to bestow on the Samaritan woman that living water the drinking of which causes one to thirst no more, and to walk on the surface of the sea with feet that do not sink, and to bring down the uplifted waves by rebuking the tempest, all this is unquestionably divine.

As then, to omit many other examples, it does not belong to the same nature to weep with feelings of pity over a dead friend and to raise that same friend from the dead with a word of power after the stone has been removed from the grave where he has lain four days, or to hang on the wood and to make all the elements tremble after day has been turned into night, or to be pierced with nails and to open the gates of paradise to the faith of the robber, so it does not belong to the same nature to say: "I and the Father are one" and "The Father is greater than I." For although in the Lord Jesus Christ the same one person is God and human, yet the principle whereby indignity belongs to both is one thing and the principle whereby glory attaches to both is another; for from us he has the humanity inferior to the Father, and from the Father he has the divinity equal to the Father.

Accordingly, on account of this unity of person which is to be understood as existing in both the natures, we read on the one hand that the Son of Man came down from heaven inasmuch as the Son of God took flesh from that virgin of whom he was born; and conversely we say that the Son of God was crucified and buried inasmuch as he underwent this not in his actual Godhead, wherein the Only-begotten is co-eternal and consubstantial with the Father, but in the weakness of human nature. Wherefore we all in the Creed also confess that "the Only-begotten Son of God was crucified and buried," according to that saying of the apostle: "For if they had known, they would not have crucified the Lord of majesty."

Letter 28, to Flavian, 4–5: The Oecumenical Documents of the Faith, ed. T. H. Bindley (fourth edition, London, 1950), 170–171, 227–228

✠

Martin

Bishop of Tours, 397

A reading from the Life of Martin, *Bishop of Tours in the late fourth century, written by Sulpicius Severus, historian*

One day when Martin had nothing on him but his weapons and his uniform, in the middle of a winter which had been fearfully hard beyond the ordinary, so that many were dying of the intense cold, he met at the city gate of Amiens a coatless beggar. This beggar had been asking the passers-by to take pity on him but all had passed by. Then the God-filled [Martin] understood, from the fact that no one else had had pity, that this beggar had been reserved for him. But what was he to do? He had nothing with him but the cape he had on, for he had already used up what else he had in similar good works. So he took the sword he was wearing and cut the cape in two and gave one half to the beggar, putting on the rest himself again.

This raised a laugh from some of the bystanders, for he looked grotesque in the mutilated garment; but many had more sense, and sighed to think that they had not done something of the kind. Indeed, having more to give, they could have clothed the beggar without stripping themselves. And that night, in his sleep, Martin saw Christ wearing the half of his cape with which he had clothed the beggar. He was told to look carefully at the Lord and take note that it was the same garment he had given away. Then he heard Jesus say aloud to the throng of angels that surrounded him: "Martin is still only a catechumen but he has clothed me with this garment."

Our Lord himself had once said: "In doing it to one of the least

207

of these, you have done it unto me," and the Lord was only acting on his own words when he declared that he had been clothed in the person of the beggar, and he reinforced his testimony to so good a deed by graciously showing himself in the very garment that the beggar had received. [Martin] however was not puffed up with vain glory by the vision, but saw God's goodness in his own good deed. And being then twenty-two years old, he hastened to be baptized.

What Martin was like, and his greatness, after entering the episcopate, it is beyond my powers to describe. For with unswerving constancy he remained the same as before. There was the same humble heart and the same poverty-stricken clothing; and, amply endowed with authority and tact, he fully sustained the dignity of the episcopate without forsaking the life or the virtues of the monk.

For a time he occupied a cell next to the cathedral. Then, when he could no longer endure the disturbance from his many visitors, he made himself a hermitage [later called Marmoutier] about two miles from the city. The place was so secluded and remote that it had all the solitude of the desert. On one side it was walled in by the rock face of a high mountain, and the level ground that remained was enclosed by a gentle bend of the River Loire. There was only one approach to it, a very narrow one.

His own cell was built of wood, as were those of many of the others; but most had hollowed out shelters for themselves in the rock of the overhanging mountain. There were about eighty disciples there, being trained in the pattern of their most blessed master. No one possessed anything personally; everything was put into the common stock. The buying and selling which is customary with most hermits was forbidden. No craft was practiced there except that of the copyist, and that was assigned to the younger ones. The older ones were left free for prayer.

It was seldom that anyone left the cell except when they assembled at the place of worship. All received their food together after the fast was ended. No one touched wine unless forced to do so by ill-health. Most of them wore clothes of camel's hair; softer clothing was looked upon as an offense. This must be regarded as all the more remarkable because there were many among them of noble rank, who had been brought up to something quite different before forcing themselves to this lowliness and endurance. Many of them we have since seen as bishops. For what kind of city or church would it be that did not covet a bishop from Martin's monastery?

Life of Martin 3; 10: The Western Fathers, transl. F. R. Hoare (London, 1954), 14–15, 23–25

NOVEMBER 12

✠

Charles Simeon
Priest, 1836

A reading from The Excellency of the Liturgy *by Charles Simeon, Priest, published in 1812*

Let us pause a moment to reflect what stress our Reformers laid on the Holy Scriptures as the only sure directory for our faith and practice and the only certain rule of all our ministrations. They have clearly given it as their sentiment that to study the word of God ourselves, and to open it to others, is the proper labour of a minister; a labour that calls for all his time and all his attention: and by this zeal of theirs in behalf of the Inspired Volume they were happily successful in bringing it into general use. But if they could look down upon us at this time and see what an unprecedented zeal has pervaded all ranks and orders of men amongst us for the dissemination of that truth, which they at the expense of their own lives transmitted to us; how would they rejoice and leap for joy!

Yet, methinks, if they cast an eye upon this favoured spot [of England] and saw that, whilst the Lord Jesus Christ is thus exalted in almost every other place, we are lukewarm in his cause; and whilst thousands all around us are emulating each other in exertions to extend his kingdom through the world, we, who are so liberal on other occasions, have not yet appeared in his favour; they would be ready to rebuke our tardiness.

Edition of New York, 1813: Prayer Book Spirituality, ed. J. Robert Wright (N.Y., 1989), 444

NOVEMBER 14

✠

Consecration of Samuel Seabury
First American Bishop, Consecrated in 1784

A reading from the Discourse on the Authority of Christ's Ministers *by Samuel Seabury, First Bishop of the Episcopal Church in the U.S.A., published in 1793*

I shall show in what respects the apostles were, and all duly authorized clergymen now are, Ministers of Christ.

The authority under which the apostles acted being derived from Christ, in the exercise of it, they were his ministers, because the authority was originally and properly his, and they could act only in his name. And this authority being, by successive ordinations, continued down to this day, all duly authorized clergymen now act by it, and are therefore "the ministers of Christ."

November 14

The commission given by our Savior to his apostles just before his ascension, as it is recorded by St. Matthew, is in these words: "All power is given unto me in heaven and in earth. Go ye therefore and teach all nations, baptising them in the name of the Father, and of the Son, and of the Holy Ghost, teaching them to observe all things whatsoever I have commanded you, and lo, I am with you always even unto the end of the world. Amen." Which may be expressed in the following manner: "Behold, in the execution of this commission I will, by my spirit and power, be present with you and your successors, even unto the consummation of all things."

On this commission is the authority of ministers in Christ's church founded, and no man can justly claim any power in spiritual matters but as it is derived from it. No one will now pretend to have received his commission to preach the gospel immediately from Christ, as the eleven apostles had theirs; and none but enthusiasts will pretend to be empowered for that work by immediate revelation from heaven, as St. Paul was. It remains then, that there is no other way left to obtain a valid commission to act as Christ's minister, in his church, but by an uninterrupted succession of ordinations from the apostles. Where this is wanting, all spiritual power in Christ's church is wanting also; while they who have any part of this original commission communicated to them, are properly Christ's ministers, because they act in his name and by authority derived from him.

All duly authorized clergymen are "the ministers of Christ," as they are the appointed rulers and governors of his church, under him the supreme and all powerful head.

One branch of that fulness of power which was given to Christ in heaven and earth, was to be the head of the church, which is stiled his body. This implies the power of instituting its government, enacting its laws, and appointing its governors to preside over it and regulate its economy, during his absence. That he did exercise this power and did delegate it to his apostles and their successors, just before his ascension into heaven, is plain from the words of the commission he gave them. If he was to be with his apostles "even unto the end of the world," their successors must have been included in the promise, for the apostles continued not beyond the ordinary term of human life.

In St. John's gospel, the commission of Christ to his apostles is thus introduced, "As my Father hath sent me, even so send I you." As, therefore, he under the power of the Father sent his apostles to be the governors of his church, so he gave them power under him to send others with the same power of governing and sending, in order to perpetuate the succession of apostolic powers to the end of the world.

From ecclesiastical history it appears that the government and officers instituted by them do continue in their successors at this present time, notwithstanding the utmost force of persecution which the malice of evil men and wicked spirits could bring upon it. Though in some places veiled in poverty and obscurity, in others encumbered with worldly pomp and ceremonious superstition, the church of Christ still continues in the world, preserved by his providence, who promised that "the gates of hell shall not prevail against it."

Discourses on Several Subjects (N.Y., 1793), vol. 1, 4–7

Additional or Alternative reading from An Earnest Persuasive to Frequent Communion by Samuel Seabury, written in 1789

The general practice in this country is to have monthly Communions, and I bless God the Holy Ordinance is so often administered. Yet when I consider its importance, both on account of the positive command of Christ and of the many and great benefits we receive from it, I cannot but regret that it does not make a part of every Sunday's solemnity. That it was the principal part of the daily worship of the primitive Christians all the early accounts inform us. And it seems probable from the Acts of the Apostles that the

Christians came together in their religious meetings chiefly for its celebration. (*Acts* 2:42, 46; 20:7.) And the ancient writers generally interpret the petition in our Lord's prayer, "Give us this day," or day by day, "our daily bread," of the spiritual food in the Holy Eucharist. Why daily nourishment should not be as necessary to our souls as to our bodies no good reason can be given.

If the Holy Communion was steadily administered whenever there is an Epistle and Gospel appointed, which seems to have been the original intention—or was it on every Sunday—I cannot help thinking that it would revive the esteem and reverence Christians once had for it, and would show its good effects in their lives and conversations. I hope the time will come when this pious and Christian practice may be renewed. And whenever it shall please God to inspire the hearts of the Communicants of any congregation with a wish to have it renewed, I flatter myself they will find a ready disposition in their minister to forward their pious desire.

In the meantime, let me beseech you to make good use of the opportunities you have; and let nothing but real necessity keep you from the heavenly banquet when you have it in your power to partake of it.

An Earnest Persuasive to Frequent Communion (New Haven, 1789), 27–28: Prayer Book Spirituality, ed. J. Robert Wright (N.Y., 1989), 324–325

NOVEMBER 16

✠

Margaret

Queen of Scotland, 1093

A reading from the Life of Margaret, *Queen of Scotland in the later eleventh century, by Turgot, Bishop of St. Andrews, who was her Confessor*

We need not wonder that Queen Margaret governed herself and her household wisely when we know that she herself acted always under the wisest of masters, the guidance of the Holy Scriptures. I myself have had frequent opportunities of admiring in her how, even amidst the distractions of lawsuits, amidst the countless cares of state, she devoted herself with remarkable attention to the word of God. Journeying thus onwards toward the heavenly country in thought and word and deed, this devout and God-worthy queen called on others to accompany her in the undefiled way, so that they with her might attain true happiness. Thus it came to pass that this venerable queen, who (by God's help) had been so desirous to cleanse God's house from all filth and error, was found day by day worthier of becoming God's temple, as the Holy Spirit shone ever brighter in her heart. Of all living persons whom I know or have known she was the most devoted to prayer and fasting, to works of mercy and almsgiving.

Let me speak first of all about her prayerfulness. In church no one was so silent and composed as she, no one so wrapt in prayer. While she was in the house of God she would never speak of worldly matters or do anything which savored of the earth; she was there simply to pray, and in praying, to pour forth her tears. Only her body was then located here below; her spirit was near to God, for in the purity of her prayer she sought nothing but God and the

214

things which belong to God. As for her fasting, I will say only this, that the strictness of her abstinence brought upon her a very severe infirmity. To these two excellent gifts of prayer and abstinence she joined the gift of mercy, for what could be more compassionate than her heart? Who could be more gentle than she toward those in need? Not only would she have given to the poor all that she possessed, but if she could have done so she would have given away her very self. She was poorer than any of the paupers; for they, even when they had nothing, wished to have something; while her desire was even to disperse the things that she had.

Vita Margaritae auctore Theodorico vel secundum alios Turgoto, 11, 17–18: Pinkerton's Lives of the Scottish Saints, ed. W. M. Metcalfe (2 vols, Paisley, 1889), vol. 2, pp. 165, 171–172

N O V E M B E R   1 7

✠

Hugh
Bishop of Lincoln, 1200

A reading from the Great Life of Hugh, *Bishop of Lincoln in the later twelfth century, written by Adam, Monk of Eynsham*

It is impossible adequately to record among the other marks of his devotion. Hugh's great compassion and tenderness toward the sick, and even to those afflicted with leprosy. He used to wash and dry their feet and kiss them affectionately, and having refreshed them with food and drink give them alms on lavish scale. He often did this privately to thirteen patients in his chamber with few people present, when that number could be found in the place where he was. There were hospitals on certain of the episcopal manors, where many men and women afflicted by this disease were maintained. He made a practice of giving gifts of many different kinds to these in addition to the revenue already assigned to them by his predecessors, and frequently visited them himself with a few of his more God-fearing and devout retainers. He would sit in their midst in a small inner room and would comfort their souls by his kindly words, relieving their sorrow by his motherly tenderness, and encouraging those who were so desolate and afflicted in this life to hope for an eternal reward, combining with amazing gentleness words of consolation and exhortations to good conduct. Also if he noticed any tendency to wrong-doing, he would exhort them not to give way to it, and if they had done so to repent, and from henceforth neither to dare nor desire to do wrong.

Those seemed to him the more beautiful who outwardly were the most horribly diseased. For this reason he declared such to be blessed, and called them the flowers of paradise and lucent pearls in the crown of the eternal king. These, he said, could confidently await the coming of our Savior Jesus Christ who would transform their vile bodies into the glory of his risen body.

Magna Vita Sancti Hugonis 4, 3: ed. Decima L. Douie and Hugh Farmer (2 vols., London, 1961–1962), vol. 2, pp. 12–14

NOVEMBER 18

✠

Hilda

Abbess of Whitby, 680

A reading from the Ecclesiastical History of England *by Bede the Venerable, Priest and Monk of Jarrow, concerning Hilda, Abbess of Whitby in the mid-seventh century*

In the following year, that is the year of our Lord 680, Hilda, abbess of the monastery of Whitby, a most religious servant of Christ, after an earthly life devoted to the work of heaven, passed away to receive the reward of a heavenly life on the seventeenth of November at the age of sixty-six. Her life on earth fell into two equal parts. She spent thirty-three years most nobly in secular occupations, and then dedicated the ensuing thirty-three even more nobly to our Lord in the monastic life.

She established the same regular life at Whitby as in her former monastery, and taught the observance of righteousness, mercy, purity, and other virtues, but especially peace and charity. After the example of the primitive Church, no one there was rich, no one was needy, for everything was held in common and nothing was considered to be anyone's personal property. So great was her prudence that not only ordinary folk, but kings and princes used to come and ask her advice in their difficulties, and take it. Those under her direction were required to make a thorough study of the Scriptures and occupy themselves in good works, to such good effect that many were found fitted for Holy Orders and the service of God's altar.

Christ's servant Abbess Hilda, whom all her acquaintances called "Mother" because of her wonderful devotion and grace, was not only an example of holy life to members of her own community. She also brought about the amendment and salvation of many living at a distance, who heard the inspiring story of her industry and goodness.

Ecclesiastical History 4, 23: Colgrave and Mynors, 404–411

NOVEMBER 19

✠

Elizabeth

Princess of Hungary, 1231

A reading from a letter by Conrad of Marburg, Spiritual Director of Princess Elizabeth of Hungary, who died in 1231

Elizabeth's goodness greatly increased. She was a lifelong friend of the poor and gave herself entirely to relieving the hungry. She ordered that one of her castles should be converted into a hospital in which she gathered many of the weak and feeble. She generously gave alms to all who were in need, not only in that place but in all the territories of her husband's empire. She spent all her own revenue from her husband's four principalities, and finally sold her luxurious possessions and rich clothes, for the sake of the poor.

Twice a day, in the morning and in the evening, Elizabeth went to visit the sick. She personally cared for those who were particularly repulsive. To some she gave food, to others clothing; some she carried on her own shoulders, and performed many other kindly services. Her husband, of happy memory, gladly approved of these charitable works. Finally, when her husband died, she sought the highest perfection. Filled with tears, she implored that she be allowed to beg for alms from door to door.

On Good Friday of that year, when the altars had been stripped, she laid her hands on the altar in a chapel in her own town, where she had established the Friars Minor, and before witnesses she voluntarily renounced all worldly display and everything that our Savior in the Gospel advises us to abandon. Even then she saw that she could still be distracted by the cares and worldly glory which had surrounded her while her husband was alive. Against my will she followed me to Marburg. Here in the town she built a hospice where she gathered together the weak and the feeble. There she attended the most wretched and contemptible at her own table.

Before her death I heard her confession. When I asked what should be done about her goods and possessions, she replied that anything which seemed to be hers belonged to the poor. She asked me to distribute everything except one worn-out dress in which she wished to be buried. When all this had been decided, she received the Body of our Lord. Afterward, until vespers, she spoke often of the holiest things she had heard in sermons. Then she devoutly commended to God all who were sitting near her, and as if falling into a gentle sleep, she died.

Ad pontificem anno 1232: A. Wyss (Leipzig, 1879), 31–35

NOVEMBER 20

✠

Edmund

King of East Anglia, 870

A reading from the Life of Edmund, *King of East Anglia, who was martyred by the Danes in 870, written by Aelfric, Abbot of Eynsham*

Edmund the blessed, king of the East Angles, was wise and honorable and, by his excellent conduct, ever glorified Almighty God. He was humble and devout, and always mindful of the counsel that if you are made a chief, do not exalt yourself but be among the people as one of them. He was bountiful to the poor and to widows, even like a father, benignly guiding his people toward righteousness, controlling the violent, and living happily in the true faith.

At last the Danes came with a fleet, harrying and slaying widely over the land. They landed in Northumbria, wasted the land, and slew the people. Hingwar, one of their leaders, sent a threatening message to King Edmund, who, undismayed, turned to the messenger and said: "Truly you deserve to die, but I will not defile my clean hands with your foul blood, because I follow Christ who has given us an example. Depart now quickly, and say to your cruel lord: Edmund the king will never bow in life to Hingwar the heathen leader, unless he will in faith first bow, in this land, to Jesus Christ." The messenger, leaving quickly, met the bloodthirsty Hingwar on the way with all his army hurrying to Edmund, and told that wicked man how he was answered. Hingwar then arrogantly commanded his troops that they should take the king who had despised his command and instantly bind him.

Edmund stood within his hall, mindful of the Savior, and threw away his weapons, desiring to imitate the example of Christ. Then those wicked men bound Edmund, shamefully insulted him and beat him with clubs, and afterward they led the faithful king to a tree, tied him to it with hard bonds, and scourged him, while with true faith he called between the blows on Jesus Christ. The heathen were madly angry, because he called on Christ to help him. They shot at him with javelins as if for their amusement, until he was covered with their shots, as with a porcupine's bristles, just as Sebastian was. When Hingwar, the wicked seaman, saw that the noble king would not deny Christ but with steadfast faith called upon him, he commanded them to behead him, and while he was

220

still calling upon Christ, the heathen drew away the saint and with one blow struck off his head; and his soul departed joyfully to Christ.

Passion of Saint Edmund, King and Martyr, 13–126: Aelfric's Lives of the Saints, ed. W.W. Skeat (EETS 114, London, 1890), 315–323; Aelfric, Lives of Three English Saints, ed. G. I. Needham (London, 1966) lines 13–107, pp. 43–50

NOVEMBER 23

✠

Clement
Bishop of Rome, c. 100

A reading from the First Letter to the Corinthians *by Clement, Bishop of Rome at the end of the first century.*

We are bound to do in an orderly fashion all that the master has bidden us to do at the appointed times. He ordered sacrifices and liturgies to be performed, and required this to be done not in a careless and disorderly way but at the times and seasons he fixed. Where he wants them performed and by whom, he himself has determined, so that everything should be done in a holy way and with his approval and should be acceptable to his will. Those therefore who make their sacrifices at the time set, win his approval and blessing, for they follow the master's orders and do no wrong. The high priest is given his particular liturgies, the priests are assigned their special place, while on the levites particular duties are imposed. The layperson is bound by the code for laity.

Each of us in our own order must please God in good conscience, not overstepping the fixed rules laid down for our ministry, but performing reverently. Not everywhere but only in Jerusalem are the different sacrifices offered—the daily ones, the freewill offerings, and those for sins and trespasses. And even there sacrifices are not offered at every place, but only in front of the sanctuary, at the altar, after the offering has been inspected by the high priest and the ministers mentioned. Those, further, who act in any way at variance with his will, incur the death penalty. Understand please, the more knowledge we are given, the greater the risk we run.

The apostles received the Gospel for us from the Lord Jesus Christ, and Jesus the Christ was sent from God. So Christ is from God and the apostles are from Christ. Thus in both instances the proper order depended upon the will of God. And so the apostles, after receiving their orders and being fully convinced by reason of the resurrection of our Lord Jesus Christ and assured by God's word, went out in the confidence of the Holy Spirit to preach the good news that God's kingdom was about to come. They preached from country to country and from city to city, and appointed their first converts, after testing them by the Spirit, to be the bishops and deacons of future believers. Nor was this an innovation, for bishops and deacons had been written of long before. For this is what Scripture says somewhere: "I will appoint their bishops in righteousness and their deacons in faith" [cf. Isaiah 60.17].

And our apostles knew through our Lord Jesus Christ that there would be strife over the title of bishop. It was for this reason and because they had been given an accurate knowledge of the future that they appointed those mentioned above and afterward added a stipulation that if these should die other approved men should succeed to their ministry. In the light of this, we view it as a breach of justice to remove from their ministry those who were appointed either by them or later on by other men of proper standing with the consent of the whole church, and who, long enjoying everyone's approval, have ministered to Christ's flock blamelessly, humbly, quietly, and unselfishly. For we shall be guilty of no slight sin if we eject from the episcopate those who have offered the sacrifices with innocence and holiness. Happy indeed are those presbyters who have already passed on, and who ended a life of fruitfulness with their task complete, for they need not fear that anyone will remove them from the place established for them.

First Letter to the Corinthians 40–42, 44: Loeb 1, 76–81, 83–85

NOVEMBER

✠

Thanksgiving Day

A reading from the original proclamation of the first nationwide Thanksgiving Day, issued in October of 1789 by George Washington, Anglican churchman and first President of the United States

Whereas it is the duty of all Nations to acknowledge the providence of Almighty God, to obey his will, to be grateful for his benefits, and humbly to implore his protection and favor. And whereas both Houses of Congress have, by their joint Committee requested me "to recommend to the People of the United States a day of public thanksgiving and prayer to be observed by acknowledging with grateful hearts the many and signal favors of Almighty God, especially by affording them an opportunity peaceably to establish a form of government for their safety and happiness."

Now therefore I do recommend and assign Thursday the 26th day of November next to be devoted by the People of these States to the service of that great and glorious Being, who is the beneficent Author of all the good that was, that is, or that will be. That we may then all unite in rendering unto him our sincere and humble thanks, for his kind care and protection of the People of this country previous to their becoming a Nation; for the signal and manifold mercies, and the favorable interpositions of his providence, which we experienced in the course and conclusion of the late war; for the great degree of tranquillity, union, and plenty, which we have since enjoyed; for the peaceable and rational manner in which we have been enabled to establish constitutions of government for our safety and happiness, and particularly the national One now lately instituted; for the civil and religious liberty with which we are blessed, and the means we have of acquiring and diffusing useful knowledge; and in general for all the great and various favors which he hath been pleased to confer upon us.

And also that we may then unite in most humbly offering our prayers and supplications to the great Lord and Ruler of Nations and beseech him to pardon our national and other transgressions; to enable us all, whether in public or private stations, to perform our several and relative duties properly and punctually; to render our national government a blessing to all the People, by constantly being a government of wise, just, and constitutional laws, discreetly and faithfully executed and obeyed; to protect and guide all Sovereigns and nations (especially such as have shown kindness unto us) and to bless them with good government, peace, and concord; To promote the knowledge and practice of true religion and virtue, and the encrease of science among them and Us; and generally to grant unto all mankind such a degree of temporal prosperity as he alone knows to be best.

Given under my hand at the City of New York the third day of October in the year of our Lord 1789.

Washington Papers, CCXLIV; Writings of Washington, ed. Sparks, XII, 119–120; Annals of Congress, 25 September 1789: Religious References in the Writings, Addresses, and Military Orders of George Washington, n.d. (Washington, 1932), 9–10

✠

James Otis Sargent Huntington
Priest and Monk, 1935

A reading from an essay written in 1933 by James Otis Sargent Huntington, Priest and Monk of the Order of the Holy Cross, which he founded

Has what is known as "The Religious Life" a legitimate place in the Church?

As to that, there are different opinions. To some persons such a life seems to be the fairest burgeoning of Christian discipleship. By others it has been regarded as a perversion of the Christian ideal in a morbid asceticism, and a false, because self-centered, spirituality.

Whatever view may be taken, there is no question but that the Religious Life, as organized in communities, has been found in the historic Church from shortly after the apostolic age. The course of the Christian fellowship has been deeply affected by it, and without it would have had a very different history, in many ages and lands. The Religious Life is a fact to be reckoned with in any comprehensive account of the Church and of civilization.

This article does not attempt to deal with the question as to whether the Religious Life has been a help or a hindrance to Christian Faith and morals, or whether, if it has served some good purpose in the past, it is now outmoded and has become an anachronism. All that will be aimed at is to describe the first efforts to establish the Religious Life for men in the Protestant Episcopal Church in the United States of America.

Two things may, however, be said, in the way of preface, to remove misunderstanding.

Prejudice against the monastic state has arisen from the use of the very phrase "The Religious Life." This has been taken to mean that the upholders of this state mean to assert that those who associate themselves in Religious Communities surpass other Christians in piety and moral excellence. That would, of course, be shocking Phariseeism, subversive of all true humility. But the term "Religious" is not used with any such implication. It simply indicates that the duties and obligations of the monk or nun are of a religious character,—worship, prayer, meditation, intercession, etc. That is their business or *métier*. If they sincerely fulfil their vocation they are doing that which will unite the soul with God. That is not true of many useful professions. A man may be a skillful physician and yet live apart from God. A man may be an honest and upright merchant and yet never say a prayer or exercise faith in God. But a "Religious" cannot discharge the duties of his calling without entering into converse with his Maker. That is why he is said to be in the "Religious State," although, alas, he may have the outward marks of a "Religious" and be secretly unfaithful to all that it should involve of loyalty and devotion; he may "have a name to live and be dead."

The other thing to be said is that the Religious Life is not, in its essentials, alien to the life of the faithful Christian whatever his status and work may be. The virtues of the Religious State are none other than the virtues which all followers of Christ should seek to exercise. Every Christian is called to discipline his body, his mind, and his spirit, that he may advance in the way of holiness. The "Religious" disciplines his body by a life of strictest purity in the celibate state; he disciplines his mind by embracing the condition of poverty, calling nothing his own; he disciplines his spirit by placing himself under the Rule of his Community, and acting in accordance with the will of his Superior. In this he is seeking to carry out, under special conditions, the programme incumbent on all Christians. All souls are commanded to seek perfection: the "Religious" vows to use certain means which, he believes, have been indicated by divine instruction and witnessed to through centuries of experience as conducive to that adventure.

"Beginnings of the Religious Life for Men in the American Church," Historical Magazine of the Protestant Episcopal Church 2:1 (March 1933), 35–36

NOVEMBER 28

✠

Kamehameha and Emma
King and Queen of Hawaii, 1864, 1885

A reading from the English translation of the Explanatory Introduction to the original Hawaiian edition of the Book of Common Prayer, written by King Kamehameha IV in 1862–63

This Book is a Book of Prayer, sanctioned by the Church of Christ as an assistant to devotion. Thus has the Church done from the earliest days, and what this book contains has reference to worship only. Its purpose is to teach men the way to pray truly to God; to point out all the rites sanctioned by His Church; the way in which those rites and the sacramental offices are to be observed and performed; to explain the fasts and holydays ordained by the Church, and to teach the priests of God their own particular functions and those things which they have together with the congregation to perform in the sight of God; to make one voice of prayer and supplication common to all, and so to establish the method and the words even of adoration that men need not only then worship in common when they worship in one congregation. This unison in adoration is no new thing, indeed it is very old; nor does it conflict in any way with the Word of God, because therein lie the prototypes of what this Church system is. Let us look to Moses and Miriam and the daughters of Israel; to Aaron with his sons, when they blessed the people; to Deborah also and to Barak: and who will deny the purposed composition of the Psalms of David as so many prayers and songs of praise to be offered, in reading or from memory, to Jehovah his God? The thanksgivings and the prayers of the Israelites down to the time of the Jews in Jerusalem, and even to the advent of our Saviour Jesus Christ, were designedly composed, not left to the inspiration of the occasion; the sentiment and the words in which the sentiment was conveyed were prepared beforehand and selected as being most seeming to the effort made by man to pay homage to his Maker; and the ceremonials before the altar, as well as those others outside of the temple and within, were all performed according to a pre-ordained rule and understanding. Our Lord Himself was not indifferent to these things while sojourning here on earth, but rather when He saw that the Jews neglected to observe some of these ancient rites He was troubled and "rebuked them."

Yet He, the Teacher Divine, from whom we date as from a new beginning of the world, did not merely follow the mode of worship as established before His day of humiliation here on earth; He, on the other hand, Himself ordained a new form of worship to be used in the place of the old, and which recognized Him. At that time, when He was finally about to soar higher than the law which He came to fulfil and to supplant, He taught His disciples saying, "When ye pray, *say,* 'Our Father which is in Heaven'," &c. The prayer which He taught was very similar to the prayer then in use among the Jews—a prayer that was rather modified than originated at that time. At the time, also, when He proclaimed Himself the Head of the New Church of which He also was the foundation-stone—while He was establishing and organizing it, the Church, before His return to Heaven whence He came, He ordained the

Apostles selected to be the guardians of that Church, and after they had received from Him the power to bind and to loose; He told them "to agree beforehand" as to what they should ask. (Matt. xviii. 19.) In many places in the Word of God we are shown how established a thing it is that the Lord is to be worshipped in this way, that is to say, by offering our praise in one voice, by singing hymns in common, by saying prayers already prepared that all may pray in concert.

But it must be remembered that what this book contains is not intended solely for the purposes of public worship. This is a book for every day and every hour of the day. It is for the solitary one and for the family group; it asks for blessings in this world as well as in the world to come; that we may be guarded from all manner of harm, from all kinds of temptations, from the power of lust, from bodily suffering, and also that we may find forgiveness of our sins. The Church has not left us to go by one step from darkness into the awful presence and brightness of God, but it has prepared for our use prayers to meet the necessities of every soul, whether they be used in public or in private.

Such is the general character of this Book of Common Prayer now offered to the people of Hawaii.

Honolulu, 1863; London, 1864; Philadelphia, 1865: reprinted Honolulu, 1955, with introductory note by Meiric K. Dutton

Acknowledgments

✠

CHURCH HYMNAL CORPORATION, New York. From *Prayer Book Spirituality,* (1989) pp. 23–25, 324, 325, 444. From *Lesser Feasts and Fasts 1991,* (1992) p. 320.

COLUMBIA UNIVERSITY PRESS, New York. From *History of the Archbishops of Hamburg-Bremen,* (1959) Adam of Bremen pp. 22–23.

DAUGHTERS OF ST. PAUL. From *The Office of Readings,* (1983) pp. 22–23, 1338–1339, 1345–1346, 1438–1439, 1485–1486, 1487–1488, 1508, 1532–1533, 1592–1593, 1636–1637.

HARVARD UNIVERSITY PRESS, Cambridge, MA. From *The Teaching of St. Gregory,* (1970) Robert W. Thomson, pp. 94–96, 106.

OXFORD UNIVERSITY PRESS, New York. From *The Oxford Movement,* (1964) Eugene R. Fairweather, pp. 39–47.

PAULIST PRESS, New York. From *The Country Parson, The Temple,* (1981) John N. Wall, p. 300. From *Divine Poems, Sermons, Devotions,* and *Prayers,* (1987) John Booty, pp. 271–272. From *A Serious Call to a Devout and Holy Life,* (1978) Paul G. Stanwood, pp. 47–50.

PENGUIN BOOKS, Baltimore, MD. From *Revelations of Divine Love,* (1966) Clifton Wolters, pp. 103–104, 110–111. From *A History of the English Church and People,* (1955) Leo Sherley-Price, pp. 33, 45–47, 68–71, 145–147, 148–149, 197–198, 204, 206, 245–248, 259, 262–264, 283, 336, 338.

ST. VLADIMIR'S SEMINARY PRESS, Crestwood, NY. From *St. Basil the Great On the Holy Spirit,* (1980) David Anderson, pp. 61–62.

UNIVERSITY OF CHICAGO PRESS, Chicago. From *St. Nicholas of Myra, Bari, and Manhattan,* (1978) Charles W. Jones, pp. 19, 63.

Index

✠

Each number refers to the page upon which a reading begins. Major Feasts from the Book of Common Prayer (1979) are shown in italics and cross-indexed to *Readings for the Daily Office from the Early Church* (RDOEC), ed. J. Robert Wright (Church Hymnal Corporation, 1991), where appropriate selections will be found. Hymns that can be used as alternate readings are cross-indexed from *The Hymnal 1982* (H1982).

Index

Index

Index

234